Being A Dad

Being A Dad

◆

The Stuff No One Told Me

Dale Alderman

iUniverse, Inc.
New York Lincoln Shanghai

Being A Dad
The Stuff No One Told Me

iUniverse, Inc.

For information address:
iUniverse, Inc.
2021 Pine Lake Road, Suite 100
Lincoln, NE 68512
www.iuniverse.com

ISBN: 0-595-29617-3 (pbk)
ISBN: 0-595-66029-0 (cloth)

Printed in the United States of America

To Starla, Chase, and Logan,
with all my love.

Contents

Introduction

I love being a dad. My boys make me laugh every day. Chase, my seven-year-old son, is already much smarter than I am. Logan, a turbocharged three-year-old, has a thousand-watt smile and a burning desire to be a superhero. Both boys are goofballs, just like me, and I love them more than they will ever know.

My wife, Starla, should receive an American Medal for Bravery to honor her courageous attempt to shape us into civilized human beings. I don't know how she puts up with the boys and me. Living with us is like sharing a home with three wild chimpanzees—we're loud, we scratch a lot, and we drop hair all over the bathroom floor.

Fatherhood brings a wealth of responsibility, but no one tells you the things you really need to know to function effectively in the most important role you will ever have in your life. To be a dad, no experience is necessary and no training is required. You have to get a license to get married, cut someone's hair, and catch a fish, but any wingnut with a fully operational assemblage of biological plumbing can father a child. You have to pass a written test to drive a car, and you have to take a class to sell a piece of real estate. However, if you want to bring another human being into the world, just go ahead and knock yourself out, Sparky; you can figure it out as you go.

I'll freely admit, when Chase was born, I didn't have a clue how to take care of a child. Oh sure, I read *What To Expect When You're Expecting*, and I went to all the child care classes Starla asked me to attend. But no one told me about the really important things (technical term: "stuff") I needed to know—like when a toddler throws a baseball, there is a 93.74% probability it will smack you in the groin. I had to acquire these critical nuggets of information the old-fashioned way: through lots of trials and many errors. As you will see in the pages ahead, I had no idea fatherhood would be this challenging or this funny.

All of the chapters in this book are based on actual events that have occurred over the past seven years. My boys were kind enough to provide me with a wealth of comic material as we laughed our way from one wacky incident to the next. I give you my word of honor as a gentleman that every word of every chapter is absolutely true, except for the stuff I made up.

This book is not an insightful guide to the mysteries of fatherhood or an enlightening exploration of the meaning of life from a dad's point of view. It's not a self-help doctrine that will alter the course of your life. I don't expect you to join a wacko religion called Daddyism, beat on drums for seven days straight, and get in touch with your inner child. This book is simply an assortment of funny stories about my life as a dad.

I'm not a medical doctor, psychologist, or psychiatrist. No one would ever confuse me with Dr. Phil—he's taller. I don't profess to be an expert in early childhood development or a professional parental counselor. I'm just a regular guy who loves his family.

Thanks for buying my book. I hope you like it. Now, let's have some fun.

Breast Pads and Nipple Cream

I still have vivid memories of the birth of my first son. Our baby was two weeks late. For some reason, that little rascal didn't want to come out of his comfortable kiddie condo, so we had to induce labor. Was something wrong with the baby? Did my wife, Starla, have an undiagnosed physical problem that was suppressing labor? My overactive imagination turned my stomach into a gooey ball of nerves.

For five years, Starla worked as a labor and delivery nurse. She's a seasoned medical professional who helped hundreds of women push their way through childbirth. I kept telling myself I would be fine during the delivery because she would have everything under control and would know exactly what to expect.

Driving to the hospital for the induction, Starla turned to me with terror in her eyes and said, "Oh, my God! I'm the Mommy! I've never been the Mommy before. I'm not qualified to do this. Turn this car around and take me home." Uh-oh.

As we worked our way through the induction process, I tried to calm myself by watching a machine I called the pain-o-graph (bad choice of words—I know that now). This machine displayed a graphical representation of Starla's contractions. Fascinating technology. I thought I was being helpful by informing her, "Honey, here comes another contraction." To which she replied, "Yes, I know" in a Linda Blair/*Exorcist* kind of voice that gave me the willies.

During the 16 hours of grueling labor (well, grueling for Starla; every couple of hours, I went to get a giant Snickers), it seemed like every person in the hospital came by to check on her progress. Doctors, interns, registered nurses, licensed practical nurses, people who wanted to be nurses, administrative staff, electricians, plumbers, computer programmers, everyone came by for an examination. They all told us the same thing, "You're only three centimeters dilated. You've got a long way to go."

We had a problem: a big baby trapped inside a little woman. Dr. Janet Glenn called the problem something, something, (oh, how the heck should I know what it was) and said, "This baby's not coming out on its own. We need to do a C-section."

A flurry of medical people flooded the room and prepped Starla for surgery. Dr. Glenn looked at me and asked, "Do you want to be in the operating room for the surgery?"

"Yes," I said, knowing that was the right answer—politically.

"Have you ever observed an operation?"

"I watch *ER* almost every Thursday night, unless there's a college football game on ESPN."

Dr. Glenn called out instructions to a labor and delivery nurse. "OK, let's get Mr. Alderman a gown and an emesis basin."

"What's an emesis basin?" I asked, knowing the answer would not be pleasant.

"A throw-up bucket."

"Good idea."

The nurse guided me into the operating room and sat me down next to Starla's face. She explained everything that was going to happen, but I couldn't comprehend a single word the nurse said. It was like my brain was locked on one thought: *I have no idea what this is going to look like, but I bet it's gonna be incredibly oogie.* I was right.

Dr. Glenn made a precise incision through Starla's abdomen (which absolutely freaked me out) and then used two large silver retractors to stretch her skin into another zip code. It looked like an experiment on the *X-Files.*

By this point, my head was spinning out of control. I kept saying moronic things like, "You're doing great, Honey," and "It will be over soon." This was coming from a guy who blew chunks when he tried to dissect a frog in the ninth grade.

The doctor pulled the baby's head up through the incision. It looked like a bizarre biological jack-in-the-box. A nurse sucked a lot of goo (I'm sure it has a medical name, but I'm going with goo) out of the baby's mouth, and Dr. Glenn pulled our new son, Chase, out of his safe sanctuary into a cold, sterile operating room. Man, was he mad. Can't blame him. He had been yanked out of his nice warm home into a freezing room filled with strangers, and he was stark naked and covered with slimy gunk—sounds like a *Fear Factor* stunt.

For the next two days, the hospital staff tried to teach me everything I needed to know about taking care of a baby…which I completely forgot as soon as we got home. We had been in the house for approximately three minutes when Starla said, "You need to go to the store and get me some breast pads and nipple cream."

"Why?"

"Because when a woman breast feeds a baby, the breasts tend to leak, so you need breast pads. After a few feedings, the nipples get raw, crack, and sometimes bleed. Nipple cream helps them heal." *Note to self—don't ever ask why.*

We were now squarely in the middle of "no one told me about this" territory. I thought she was yanking my chain. What kind of store would have these items? Breast Pads 'n Things? I didn't have a clue, so I went to my friendly neighborhood Super Wal-Mart (you can't hide money).

Standing in the health and beauty aid aisle, I realized I needed to move fast so no one would see me buying feminine products. I quickly grabbed a supersized package of breast pads and the biggest jar of nipple cream I could find. Like a rocket…well, not like a rocket…like a…um…a walrus in a really big hurry, I ran to a checkout lane.

I stood in line and tried to act manly by looking at the Britney Spears magazine covers (yes, OK, I do that in every store; give me a break). I casually put my items on the checkout conveyor and tried to keep a low profile. The chucklehead in front of me didn't believe any of the prices generated by the register and demanded price checks for a hammer, a Stone Cold Steve Austin lunch bucket, and a bag of pork rinds. This process was going to take forever. Five more people joined me to wait in the checkout line.

For some unknown reason, a lady who was wearing a yellow Tweety Bird tee shirt and was standing in line behind me felt the need to announce, "Lansinoh is the best nipple cream."

"What?" Flop sweat began to pour out of every pore in my body.

"You must have picked up this cheapo generic nipple cream by mistake. Everyone knows Lansinoh is the best kind of nipple cream. It's the only nipple cream that doesn't have preservatives, and it contains the world's purest lanolin." I ignored the Tweety woman because I was too embarrassed to engage her in a public conversation about nipple cream.

After what seemed to be 30 hours of painful anticipation, it was finally my turn to purchase my feminine products. Maude the checkout lady, a 57-year-old hunka hunka burnin' love, looked at my items and said, "You know, Hon, you picked up the wrong kind of nipple cream. Lansinoh is the best you can buy. My youngest daughter is 28 years old, and I still use it. Sometimes on Saturday night, my husband, Elrod, grabs a big handful of Lansinoh and…."

"OK, OK, I'm in a real hurry here. Can you please ring me up?" *Shoot me now.*

"I told him Lansinoh is the best kind of nipple cream, but he ignored me," the Tweety woman whined.

"When Elrod ignores me, I withhold sex."

"That's it. I'm outta here." I threw a wad of cash toward the register and ran out of the store as fast as my bad knees would take me.

I still felt nauseous when I got home. I put the feminine items in the bathroom hoping never to hear about them again and made my way to the TV. Certainly, *Xena: Warrior Princess* could help me forget about this awful experience.

I had just plopped my big butt in my recliner when Starla said in a chilling voice, "Dale, you got the wrong kind of nipple cream. You need to go back and get some Lansinoh. Everyone knows it's the best kind."

The Hooter Fairy

About five to seven days after a baby is born, a most wonderful event occurs: the fabulous Hooter Fairy pays her first visit to the new mother. Although no one has actually seen the Hooter Fairy, my guess is she looks like Pamela Anderson. This astonishing creature delivers breast milk to the new mother and, in just a matter of hours, transforms an A cup into a C cup. Now that's what I call a great magic trick. I'd like to see David Copperfield try this one.

The typical, red-blooded male response to this blessed event is "oh, boy; oh, boy; oh, boy," but eventually, bad news rears its ugly head. This public service announcement is for all of you new and expectant dads: there are two important facts you need to know about these magnificent bundles of joy:

1. They are not for you.

2. They will go away.

Let's discuss these cruel realities in detail. Important fact number one: you must face the grim reality that they are not for you. Here is a typical situation: You're in the living room, sitting in your favorite chair, watching a very educational television show called *The Beverly Hillbillies*. Your wife has just put your newborn infant down for a nap. She walks into the living room. You notice that the amazing Hooter Fairy made an extra large deposit for the day. Your wife sits on the couch, and you mosey over to join her. You make your best move.

"What are you doing?" she says.

"I just thought we could…you know…enjoy our new additions." *Oh, yeah, smooooth. You are such a Casanova.*

"Here's a news flash, Skippy. These are for the baby—not you."

Like an idiot, you keep trying. "Come on, Honey. I love you. Really. I do."

"If your hands get any closer to me, you will draw back a pair of stumps." *Whoa, where did that come from*, you wonder.

Although breastfeeding is quite healthy for the baby, it can take its toll on the mother. Oh sure, women say it is a beautiful experience that creates a special bond between mother and child. They also say, "It hurts like hell. Stay away from me, or I'll stab you with a shrimp fork."

Many women use breast pumps to express milk for use at a later time. WARNING: Never, under any circumstance, watch a woman use a breast pump. Let's say you're sitting in your favorite chair, watching a documentary on the works of Louisa May Alcott…or maybe wrestling. You hear an unfamiliar buzzing noise and search the house for its origin. The HVAC is OK. Most important, the satellite dish is in fine working order. You track the buzzing sound to your bedroom. You slowly open the door and see your wife sitting on the bed with a grisly contraption attached to…GASP! Oh, the inhumanity. This vision will be burned into your brain permanently. Don't let this happen to you. It can be pushed into the subrecesses of your mind only with a powerful combination of beer, football, and the Oakland Raiders cheerleaders.

Some women are quite open about breastfeeding their infants in public. What if a woman plants herself on a bench at the mall and opens the baby buffet with no inhibitions? This situation is confusing for me. Am I supposed to look? I want to look, but then again, it's sort of weird in an oogie kind of way. OK, I'll look. Hey, that baby looks like Winston Churchill. Oops, she caught me looking. She probably thinks I'm a pervert. I'll just duck into the nearest store: Lane Bryant. Now she thinks I'm a cross-dresser. I'm not, but they do have a number of lovely jackets that flatter my figure.

All right, let's move on to important fact number two: they will go away. After about six months of breast feeding, the baby graduates to solid food. Mom is elated because she gets her body back. At this point, the Hooter Fairy stops making deliveries. The beautiful, bountiful blessings that were off limits to you for the past six months make a rapid departure. Like a thief in the night, the awesome C cups disappear, leaving you frustrated and depressed.

After six months of living with her temporary ample assets, Mom may become intrigued with the idea of having larger breasts. Her clothes fit differently and her body shape changed radically during this period of bosom enlightenment. She may even ask this question: "Honey, do you think I should get breast implants?"

WARNING: Do not provide an answer. This loaded question could wreak havoc in your life for the foreseeable future. It ranks right up there with other hazardous questions women ask men, such as "If something were to happen to me, would you marry a younger woman?" "Do you think my sister is pretty?" Or "How would you feel if my mother came to live with us?"

The "should I get implants" question is particularly perilous because any committed response you offer can create a losing proposition for you. For example, if you say, "Yes," she could say, "Oh, so you don't like me the way I am. You want me to become some plastic plaything for your enjoyment. Well, it's not gonna happen in your lifetime, Mister." The implant concept is immediately removed from her thought processes, and your chances of getting lucky in the next decade are nonexistent.

Some men may try to use reverse psychology and answer the implant question with a "No" response. They think their mate will take the opposing opinion and get the implants as a move of defiance. Bad idea. Reverse psychology works only on *The Brady Bunch*. If you say, "No dear, you don't need implants," she'll believe you and abandon the idea completely. Another dreadful outcome for you.

A potential response to the implant question could be, "Honey, it's your body and your decision. I will love you and support you either way."

She will probably say, "You are so full of crap," and make her own decision without your input. Not the best result, but at least you're not sleeping on the couch with only the *Sports Illustrated Swimsuit Edition* to keep you company.

If you become overly aggravated in this situation, you will need to perform an act of retribution. Go to Dunkin' Donuts. Buy a dozen double chocolate donuts, and take them home while they are still warm. Sit down directly in front of your wife and chow down. When she reaches for one of the donuts say, "There are two things you must realize about these donuts: (1) they are not for you, and (2) they will go away."

I'll Be Gone for
Only a Few Minutes

There are three things I don't want to be trapped in a room alone with: a hungry grizzly bear, a politician who is running for office, and an eight-week-old baby. These scary creatures can make my life miserable in so many ways.

For the first few weeks after Chase was born, Starla refused to take him out of the house. She didn't want him to get accosted by a pack of renegade germs on the prowl to infest defenseless newborns. She stayed close to him night and day to make sure he was safe and healthy. Although she was successful in her mission to keep our newborn out of harm's way, Starla contracted a severe case of "I've got to get the heck outta this house before I gouge my eyes out with a spoon" fever. The endless cycle of breast-feeding every three hours, changing 12 diapers a day, and sleeping 15 minutes in a 72-hour period of time shattered her nerves. This situation became dangerous. If she didn't get a break soon, she could snap and beat me senseless with a box of Huggies Baby Wipes.

After eight weeks of full-contact motherhood, on a sunny Saturday morning in August, she made the decision to break out of the joint. She handed Chase to me, looked me straight in the eye, and said, "I'm going to the grocery store—BY MYSELF!"

My heart raced. "But…that means I'll be alone with the baby. I've never been alone with an infant before. What if something happens? I won't know what to do."

"You'll be fine. I'll be gone for only a few minutes." She kissed Chase on the cheek and bolted out the door. She walked quickly to her car, stopped, looked around to see if anyone was watching, and performed a joyful dance of freedom. She looked as if she had just scored a touchdown in an NFC Championship Game. Chase suddenly realized his mother was not within his 10-foot comfort radius and burst into tears.

"Awwwww! Come on, Buddy. She's not even in the car yet." I tried to catch her before she left. I hoped she would see Chase crying and come back to console me…I mean him. When Starla saw the front door open, she leaped into the driver's seat and peeled out of the driveway like a Formula One racer. I think I heard her laughing at me as she drove out of sight. Chase was still crying. My nightmare had begun.

I racked my brain to come up with a couple of possible remedies to calm my crying infant: either he needed a change or he was hungry. I checked his diaper for a poop deposit. Clean! OK, maybe he's hungry. I took a bag of frozen breast milk from the freezer and made a nice warm bottle for him. He was still crying at the top of his lungs as we settled into the couch for his snack. He took the bottle eagerly and started to drink. We were all set to have a nice relaxing morning. I turned on the TV and searched for a *Star Trek* episode. About an ounce into the bottle, Chase made an odd gurgling noise. Five seconds later, he blew grits all over me, the couch, the coffee table, and an issue of *People Magazine* I hadn't read yet. The crying started again.

I panicked. I had explored the only two remedies I knew of and his crying was getting worse. Where was Starla? She said she would be gone for only a few minutes. I looked at the clock, and she had been gone for a whopping 10 minutes. The problem grew into a full-scale crisis. I held Chase in every possible position, walked around the house 48 times, and shook every rattle I could find at him. No luck. Still crying.

OK...um...I could sing him a song. Let's see..."Hush, little baby, don't you cry. Daddy's gonna buy you a pig that flies. If that stupid pig won't fly, Daddy's gonna poke him in the eye." More crying.

How about a trip to Funkytown? I sang songs by Chaka Khan and Stevie Wonder. No luck. The extended crying caused Chase's face to become red and splotchy. What the heck was taking Starla so long?

Just then, the television blasted a commercial for *Goin' South*, a compilation album with 35 of the biggest southern rock hits from the '70s and '80s packed into one dynamite collection. The Lynyrd Skynyrd classic "Sweet Home Alabama" blew through the television speakers like a hurricane. Chase stopped crying, and his face brightened with a huge smile. Evidently, I passed my southern rock DNA on to Chase, and he was genetically predisposed to love Skynyrd. He was blissfully content. Hey, I'm pretty good at this fatherhood business. I love being a dad!

I pulled out all of my southern rock albums, and for the next two hours, Chase and I rocked the house. We listened to Skynyrd's monster hit "Freebird" and then moved on to the Allman Brothers' "Ramblin' Man" and "Midnight Rider." I exposed Chase to some of the greatest southern rock songs ever written, such as "Flirtin' With Disaster" by Molly Hatchet, "Slow Ride" by Foghat,

"Can't You See" by the Marshall Tucker Band, "There Goes Another Love Song" by The Outlaws, and "Hold on Loosely" by .38 Special.

At the end of our southern male bonding session, Chase fell asleep in my arms. I gently placed him in his crib, and I relaxed in my recliner.

Starla walked in the door exactly three hours after her speedy departure. "I thought you were gonna be gone for only a few minutes," I said.

"I saw Joyce in the store and we chatted for a while. Were you OK with the baby? Any problems? Mishaps? Disasters? Meltdowns?"

"Nope. We had a great time together. Taking care of an infant by yourself is actually quite easy when you know what works for your child. I don't know why you think it's so difficult."

She chuckled, kissed me lightly on the cheek, and beat me senseless with a box of Huggies Baby Wipes.

I Should Wear a Cup

Before I had kids, I thought toddlers were cute, squishy, and huggable. Although they are mighty cuddly, I discovered toddlers are dangerous creatures who can inflict massive amounts of pain at any given instant. Here's a safety tip for you new dads: on your child's first birthday, run out to the nearest metal shop and buy a suit of armor. You will thank me later. Buy the one made for men with extra-sensitive skin so you won't get a rash.

When Chase was a toddler, he loved to crawl up in my lap and wrestle. We goofed around until somebody got hurt. Oops! Let me rephrase that…until I got hurt. Over the years, I've been poked in the eye with a He-Man sword, whacked in the nose with a fire engine, and smacked in the mouth with an assortment of lethal weapons ranging from matchbox cars to an astronaut's helmet. Logan constantly hits me in the teeth with the hardest object known to man: his head.

These incidents led me to perform an in-depth experiment to evaluate the clear and present danger that a toddler presents to his dad. My scientific study, conducted under a highly controlled environment (my backyard) reveals two conclusions: First, when a toddler throws a baseball to his dad from a distance greater than or equal to five feet away, he will throw the ball in a random direction. The wild pitch will force the man to fetch the ball and grunt like a pig when he bends over to pick it up. Second, when a toddler throws a baseball to his dad from less than or equal to four feet away, there is a 93.74% probability he will throw the ball at a speed of over 90 MPH like All-Star Pitcher Randy Johnson, and the round, hard projectile will smack his dad right in the groin. The wounded man will fall on the ground and cry like a little girl. I call my hypothesis The Johnson Theory.

This leads me to another safety tip for new dads: wear a protective cup at all times, even at night. You must be prepared because kids will get you when you least expect it. Don't fall asleep on the couch without your cup. A toddler will sneak up on you while you're sawing logs and konk you in the globes with a toy train.

The most dangerous armaments in a toddler's arsenal are his feet. Oh yeah, they're fat and squeezable, but a toddler can use his feet to cause an enormous amount of pain to the family jewels. Toddlers like to stand up in their dad's lap. For some reason, they think it's fun to clomp around like they're stomping bugs. The problem is their feet always land in the worst place possible, and if they are wearing shoes, Dad will be out of commission for a few hours. Why do they make kids' shoes so hard? A kid's sneaker feels like a wrecking ball when it hits you in the nuggets with 7,000 pounds of pressure behind it.

Holding your toddler on your lap is not the only hazardous situation you will encounter. Although they seem relatively safe, shopping carts can be deadly to a father. One day, when Chase was almost two years old, we went to Costco because we needed some critical items: a 20-gallon vat of mayonnaise, a pallet of toilet paper, and 12 cases of donuts. I lifted Chase into the shopping cart child seat with him facing me and made a beeline toward the Krispy Kreme section.

Along the way, I got distracted by a home theater display, a steel-belted radial tire sale, and a 19-year-old blonde in a halter top and shorts who was giving away free samples of Cheez Whiz. I ambled down the aisle toward her thinking…*oh yeah, I still got it.* Of course, I'm sure she was thinking…*what a cute little boy with that overweight, middle-aged, delusional man.* Just as I passed in front of her, Chase began kicking his feet as they dangled from the shopping cart child seat. He swung his left foot upward and cracked me in the groin with his Baby Nike.

"Would you like to try some Cheez Whiz today?" the young lady asked as she burst into laughter.

"No, but could you tell me where I could find the frozen food section," I whimpered. She pointed toward the back of the store, and I limped away in agony. I grabbed a package of frozen fries and placed them on my damaged goods to ease the pain. You know, people look at you funny when you walk through Costco holding a bag of Ore Ida Golden Crinkles on your crotch. They also move out of your way and shield their children from you.

I suffer these types of injuries all the time, even when my kids are somewhere else. A couple of weeks ago, I went to Starbucks to get a venti-mocha-lotta-cappa-drippy-thinga-dootle. Can someone tell me why the heck they have to make ordering a stupid cup of coffee so complicated? The woman in front of me picked up her two-year-old daughter to give her a hug. The toddler swung her right black patent leather shoe around her mother's waist and caught me square in the nuggets. My face took on a Wyle E. Coyote "Oh, no! I just got hit with an anvil!" expression, and I lost my breath for a few minutes.

"I'm so sorry! Why don't you go ahead of me in line?" the mom apologized as she held back a huge belly laugh.

"What can I get for you, sir?" the barista asked.
"I'll have a decaf…and a bag of Golden Crinkles."

Look Out! He's Gonna Blow!

I'm a bit squeamish. You could even say I have a delicate stomach. Let's put it this way, I can't watch the second stunt on a *Fear Factor* episode, which usually requires the contestants to eat something really disgusting like fish eyes or pig intestines or spinach. I hide my eyes. Chase has to tell me when it's over.

My biggest fear in becoming a father was dealing with the gross stuff. I have a highly pronounced gag reflex. Just thinking about disgusting things like slime, body fluids, or Roseanne Barr in a thong turns my stomach into the biological equivalent of a snow blower. Oh dear…hold on…I'll be right back…[flush].

When Starla was pregnant with Chase, I tried to bargain with her. "I'll help him with math, and you can change the diapers." No response. "I'll mow the lawn, and you can change the diapers." Again no response. "I'll kill bugs and carry heavy stuff so you can change the diapers." She hit me with a bag of frozen broccoli. It left a mark.

I succumbed to spousal pressure and tried valiantly (well, not valiantly, let's be realistic here) to change my son's diapers. I could handle number one, but number two was another story. One day, Chase was playing in his exersaucer (a toy that allows a child to sit in a circular, stationary chair and play with a bunch of different toys, while Dad watches the NBA Playoffs). An odd expression took over his face. His eyebrows reflected physical strain. Being a good father, I recognized this situation and called to my wife, "Honey, I think he's gonna need a change."

"I'm on the phone. You do it," Starla answered.

I'll just wait her out, I thought. She'll be off the phone soon, and she can deal with it. Besides, Shaq was playing Mr. Robinson in the Western Conference Finals.

A few minutes went by, and a funky smell started to waft through the air. When I say funky, I don't mean George Clinton Parliament Funkadelic funky. I mean, "Call the HAZMAT crew because this is an emergency," funky. Fearing the worst, I peered down the back of his diaper and the escaping vapors wound around my head like a swirling cloud of death.

I yelled in desperation, "Honey, I need a little help here."

"I'm still on the phone. You can do it." No way out of this one.

I held my breath and gingerly pulled Chase out of his exersaucer. The poop had defied gravity and crawled up his back. My eyes began to water and my gag reflex kicked into high gear. I fought courageously to suppress my weak stomach because I was afraid the odor would attach itself to Chase's skin permanently. I couldn't have him go through life with "Stinky" as his nickname.

I positioned him on the changing table so I would have easy access to wipes, baby powder, and ointment. When I opened his diaper, the smell was so strong it peeled paint off the walls. The stench assumed a life of its own. It killed the grass in our front yard. Skunks were offended. Every dog in a 10-mile radius ran for cover. The aroma infiltrated our carpet. We didn't need a fumigation team, we needed an exorcist.

After another occurrence of the "poop from hell," we knew something was horribly wrong, so we took Chase to see his pediatrician. He was diagnosed with something called the Rotavirus (derived from the Latin word "Rota," which means "smells worse than the floor of a chicken coop").

For seven more days, we suffered with the evil virus. We threw our trashcans away. The neighbors bought gas masks. Our garbage man billed us for hazard pay. During those seven days of adversity, every time Chase dropped a bomb, Starla claimed she was on the phone. Do you think she…nah…I'm sure it was pure coincidence.

I am convinced children have a sixth sense that identifies their most squeamish parent. I am a vomit target. No matter where I am, in the bedroom, the kitchen, or a Hampton Inn in Albuquerque, New Mexico, my kids will find a way to throw up on me.

For instance, when Chase was an infant, I gave him a bottle of milk each night before bed. He got sleepy and I watched *SportsCenter*—a classic father and son experience. Invariably, after guzzling eight ounces of milk, he would project 64 gallons of baby yak all over me, the dog, and my recliner. Our cocker spaniel, Joe, learned his lesson after being drenched a few times. He escaped upstairs when he saw me making the bottles at night. I never learned because I am a stupid, stupid man.

Later that same year, for a number of consecutive weeks, I traveled Monday through Friday to work on a project at Redstone Arsenal in Huntsville, Alabama. The people were fun and the pecan pie was awesome, but the travel sucked. I hated to be away from my family.

My flights home connected through Charlotte, North Carolina. At the time, the NFL had just launched a new expansion team in Charlotte, The Carolina

Panthers. Charlotte's airport was packed with their merchandise. The team had really cool black and blue uniforms. One night on my way home, I saw a Panther uniform for a toddler hanging in an airport store window. I had to have it for Chase. Thirty-two dollars later, I packed the uniform in my suitcase and made my way to my plane, which was delayed by four hours. I got home at midnight.

The next morning I showed the uniform to Starla. She immediately put it on Chase, handed him to me and said, "Don't move. I'm gonna get my camera. He's so cute." She ran upstairs to search for the camera.

I sat down on the couch and turned Chase to face me so I could see him in his new Panther uniform. Without any warning…bbbrrrrggghhhh. Old Faithful erupted. After wearing the Panther uniform for approximately nine seconds, he completely totaled the outfit. We replaced the couch. I burned my clothes and took three showers to get clean. Now I get queasy when I watch the Panthers play on TV.

I keep thinking my kids will outgrow this problem. No such luck. A couple of weeks ago, Logan went to a birthday party for one of his schoolmates. He consumed about 312 pounds of ice cream and then ran around like a maniac for an hour. On the way home in the car, he didn't say a word. As I unbuckled his seatbelt to get him out of the car, I noticed his face was ghostly white. I could tell he was getting ready to blow.

I cautiously escorted him inside the house. Starla was reading the newspaper in her favorite squishy chair in the living room. "Why don't you sit with Mommy for a little while? She'll make you feel better," I said. He crawled into her lap and I raced upstairs to get out of the line of fire.

Sure enough, 10 minutes later, I heard him say, "Mommy, I don't feel…bbbrrrrggghhhh."

"Can I get a little help down here?" Starla shrieked in misery.

"Sorry, Hon. I'm on the phone."

What's in a Name

Picking out a name for your child is a harrowing experience. There are a bazillion names to consider, ranging from Aaron to Ziggy. The pressure to pick a good name becomes gargantuan because your child will have to live with it for his entire life or at least until he enters the witness protection program. Some names just don't work for one reason or another, like Former Senior Advisor to the President for Policy and Strategy Skeeter Stephanopoulos, Buffy Rodham-Clinton the Vampire Slayer, or Vladimir "Corky" Putin.

Some parents neglect to think through the combination created by their favorite first name and their last name. For example, there is a professional baseball player named Milton Bradley. No kidding. What the heck went through their minds back in 1978 when the Bradley family selected this name? "You know, dear, the name Milton Bradley has a very familiar ring to it. I have a feeling he'll love to play board games." Can you imagine going through high school with a name like Milton Bradley? How many hundreds of times did he hear, "Hey, Milton, bet you're really good at Chutes and Ladders. You must be a Scrabble guru." As it turned out, Milton became an awesome athlete, and he'll probably stuff me in a gym locker for making fun of his name.

In the past few years, many people have given their children the names of states and cities, such as Georgia, Orlando, Virginia, Dakota, Austin, Montana, and Madison. If this trend continues, we'll have kids with names like Rhode Island Liebowitz, Sacramento Jones, Bucketville Baker, Beaver Falls Braselton, Idaho Gilucci, and Hoboken Gandhi.

Saddling your child with an unusual name generates an enormous amount of teasing from other children, which could possibly cause irreparable harm to the child's psyche and lead to thousands of hours of very expensive therapy. A famous illustration of this problem is Tipper Gore. Born Mary Elizabeth Aitcheson, Mrs. Gore was nicknamed Tipper by her mother. How could a mother give her daughter a name that makes her sound like a miniature schnauzer? What are her siblings called…Lassie and Rin Tin Tin? Are her cousins named Sparky, Topper, and Spot?

Flower children of the '60s thought it was cool to give their love children atypical names like Sunshine, Moonbeam, and Freedom. Forty years later, we now hear introductions such as, "Hello. My name is Dolphin Habitat Dillman, and I'll be your defense lawyer"; and "Hi. My name is Free Love Williams. I'm a senior partner with PriceWaterhouseCoopers."

Rap and hip-hop music artists have pushed the name game into uncharted territory. Only ultrahip people can walk around with names like Snoop Doggy Dog, Busta Rhymes, Lil' Bow Wow, Coolio, Gansta Boo, Ja Rule, and Ludacris. Some of their names provide a description of the rapper's physical features, like Notorious B.I.G., which could eventually lead to names like Stanky Hank and The Great S.C.H.N.O.Z.O.L.A.

Other artists take their names from everyday items. A famous abstract hip-hop poet is called Q-Tip. How far will this trend go? Will we soon see artists named Kleenex and Lestoil, or will someone take a familiar name like Clorox and spell it incorrectly to become hard core rap master Klo-Rocks?

A few artists have names that fall within a common theme such as Ice Cube, Ice-T, and Vanilla Ice. If this notion continues to flourish, pretty soon we'll see artists called Flavor-Ice, Italian Ice, Icy Hot, and Ice Shot the Sheriff.

I just became aware of a rapper named 50 Cent. Yep, that's his name…50 Cent. Can you imagine what his parents called his siblings? I bet he has two older brothers, Buck and A Quarter. His oldest brother probably goes by $19.95.

The popular rapper Eminem's real name is Marshall Mathers III…a wise name change. It's difficult to come up with a cool rap name, so if you happen to be a new artist who is looking for a hip name, I have some ideas for you. Feel free to use any of the following suggestions: Poppa Zit, Busta Gut, Cuppa Soup, Sacka Taters, Bagga Chips, Canna Whoopass, and Englebert Humperdink. You're welcome, and good luck with your recording career.

When Starla was pregnant with our youngest son, we pored over names for months, trying to find the perfect one. Some names reminded us of people we hated in high school, and others sounded like the names of geeks who were in the math club…hey, wait a minute…I was in the math club. We rejected every name we could find until one day, out of the blue, Starla said, "How about Logan?"

"That's it. The perfect name!" I exclaimed. Starla liked the name, and I thought it was exceedingly cool because one of the most exciting characters in the *X-Men* comics is also named Logan (nicknamed Wolverine). My kid would have the same name as a superhero. Oh yeah, what a great idea. I didn't tell Starla about the comic book connection because she would probably think I was being stupid. Hey, it could have been worse. I could have said, "I know, let's name him

Cyclops or Nightcrawler." As it turned out, Logan loves having the same name as an *X-Man,* and he tells everyone he meets about his affiliation with a mutant superhero.

About four months ago, Logan saw a commercial for the *X-Men* film *X2,* which features Logan (Wolverine) in a prominent role. He had to see the movie. Every day he would ask me, "Daddy, will you pleeeeeeeeze take me to see the *X-Men* movie?" I would always say, "Yes, Logan, I will take you to see the *X-Men* movie" because I really wanted to see it too.

The day the movie opened, I took Logan to catch the 2:00 PM matinee. He was so excited, he was about to burst. As we stood in line to buy our tickets, he told everyone within a 25-foot radius, "My name is Logan. I'm Wolverine." When we entered the theater, he told the ticket-taker-tearer-upper-guy, "I'm Logan. If you need me, I'll be watching the *X-Men* movie." I'm sure the guy made a note of Logan's comment. Our next mission was to acquire popcorn and drinks. We placed our order for a medium bucket of popcorn, a package of M&Ms, and two small drinks.

"That will be $28.50," said the pizza-faced teen behind the counter. His name tag said, "Hello, my name is Albert."

"Holy cow! You must have a huge profit margin built into the price of popcorn," I said. *Geez, I sound like a crotchety old man.*

"I don't know, sir. I'm not a math club geek," Albert replied with an annoyed expression on his face.

"Well, maybe you can get into the math club if you work hard. I was in the math club. In fact, Einstein's first name was Albert. Just like yours."

"Who?"

"You know…Albert Einstein…theory of relativity…$E=MC^2$…does any of this ring a bell?"

"E = MC Hammer? I'm sorry, what are you talking about, sir?"

"Never mind, Al, just give me my ridiculously overpriced popcorn, and we'll be on our way." We gently carried our gold-plated snacks into the theater and found two prime seats in preparation for the show.

Logan wolfed down the M&Ms and half of my…uh, our…popcorn before the previews started. He talked nonstop through the trailers for *The Incredible Hulk, Finding Nemo,* and *The League of Extraordinary Gentlemen.* When the *X-Men* movie finally started, he clapped his hands and cheered at the top of his lungs for his namesake, Logan, the Wolverine. He settled into his seat and leaned against my shoulder to get comfortable. Ten minutes into the movie, I realized he had become very quiet. The excitement zapped all of his energy, and the little dude was zonked out. I tried to wake him up, but once Logan is asleep, he's out for about two hours. He woke up to see the last five minutes of the movie. Luckily, since Logan is three, he thought he had seen the entire movie and was completely satisfied. Walking out of the theater, Logan saw another three-year-old and said, "My name is Logan. I'm Wolverine."

The other three-year-old replied, "My name is Bruce Banner. I'm the Hulk."

I asked his dad, "Is his name really Bruce?"

"Yes, in fact, his name really is Bruce Banner just like the main character in the *Hulk* comic books."

"Cool. His mom doesn't know about the comic book connection, does she?" I asked.

A big, goofy grin crossed his face, "Nope."

Writer's note: I understand people can be quite sensitive about their names, so if I have offended you in any way, shape, or form, you can contact my attorney, Hopalong Finklestein.

Ya Better Get This Potty Started

Why do so many kids resist potty training? For whatever reason they cook up in their young minds, a lot of kids make the potty training process long and arduous. It's like they would rather walk around with a load in their drawers than make a deposit in the porcelain poopie bank. Every child potty trains differently, but researchers believe boys tend to resist more adamantly than girls. Both of my boys proved this theory to be completely true.

When Chase was a toddler, he fully understood the concept of potty training; however, he would have no part of it. No matter how much we talked about it or how much we encouraged him, he vehemently refused to even attempt to go on the potty. We tried everything from videos to books to songs. Nothing happened.

For six months we worked to no avail, until Starla finally decided to put him in a pair of big boy underwear and let the chips fall where they may. We knew it was a crapshoot, but we rolled the dice and took our chances, hoping this dangerous idea would work. To my surprise, Chase actually responded by peeing in the potty. I never knew I could get so excited about a squirt of urine, but I danced around the house for hours when he did it the first time.

Number two was a different story. He wouldn't do it…at all. No matter how strong the urge became, no matter how long it lasted, he fought back the impulse to poop. Chase knew he couldn't go in his underwear, and he refused to go to the potty, so he suffered the consequences. He would say, "My butt hurts, but I don't have to poop," as he broke into a cold sweat. "I'm not doin' it. No way." For eight days and nights, he suppressed the poopie demons that churned inside his body. We figured sooner or later he would poop or pop. Either way, the yucky stuff was gonna come outta there.

Finally, on a Saturday morning in May, he made a command decision and went to the bathroom. It looked like a hippopotamus had broken into our house and trashed our first floor powder room. The unbelievably horrid smell permeated the walls of our house. Our dog, Joe, fainted and had to be revived with a Snausage. This 32-pound kid had dropped about 20 pounds of poop. Chase felt like a new kid and ran around the house yelling, "I'm a big boy now!"

I ran around the house yelling, "No more diapers! Yaaaaa Hooooooo!" It didn't occur to me that we would have another child, and that I would have to run this drill a second time.

Just like his brother before him, Logan refused to go along with the idea of potty training. This time, we were much smarter about the process. We just waited him out. Starla said, "No one goes to kindergarten in diapers. He'll eventually figure it out and do it when he's ready." As usual, she was right. One day, something clicked and he simply decided he was ready to go to the potty.

Now after Logan goes to the bathroom, he yells, "Dad, come here. Ya gotta see this." We have to look at the poopie before we flush. I know it's gross, but it keeps him on track with his potty training so I go along with it. Did you know that blueberries look the same going out as they do going in? I didn't.

If you are currently trying to potty train a child, you can find many helpful tips on the Internet that may work for you. One website says you can use dolls or action figures to show your child how to go to the potty. Do not use a teddy bear for this simulation. Bears poop in the woods. You don't want to encourage this type of behavior.

I have heard that some parents pick a potty day. They circle a date on a calendar that signifies the day their child will go to the potty. I wonder, what happens if he doesn't seal the deal as per their agreement? They probably penalize him $50 a day until he completes the job.

A friend of mine successfully used the warm water technique. When your child is sitting on the potty, fill a big bowl with lukewarm water. Put a few toys in the bowl and set it in front of your child. When your child places his hand in the water to get the toys, he may go to the bathroom immediately. This technique will also prepare him for his freshman year in college.

Many parents put targets in the toilet so their child can shoot at them. This tip works best for boys because girls have lousy aim. The challenge taps into the natural male interest in hitting targets. Inexpensive objects you can use for target practice include Cheerios, Fruit Loops, pictures of James Carville and Pat Buchanan, *The National Enquirer*, and a CD of William Shatner's greatest hits.

I recently heard about some imaginative parents who created a pee-pee tree. They had a boy who insisted on peeing in his underwear, so they painted a bull's-eye on a tree and let him fire away. I guess you could try this idea if you're desperate. If you don't have a tree in your yard, paint a bull's-eye on an obnoxious neighbor's Lexus.

Some child development experts say if your child protests potty training adamantly, you should allow him to run around naked. This way the child has no choice but to go to the potty. If you try this idea, be prepared to explain yourself the next time you take your kid to McDonald's.

I'm sure one day I'll look back on this time of my life and laugh at the struggle we went through to get the boys to perform a simple human activity. I'd also like to see the day in the distant future when I can visit Logan in his home, go to the bathroom, and then yell, "Hey, Logan, come here. Ya gotta see this."

Stop It, Quit It, Stop It, Quit It, Stop It, Quit It, Stop It

Three-year-olds are just plain ornery (southern term meaning "royal pain in the butt"). Don't get me wrong, I love my three-year-old, Logan, more than anything in the world, but he makes me **CRAZY AS A LOON**.

Many people say the "Terrible Twos" are unbearable; however, I speak from experience when I say the "Torturous Threes" are waaaaaaaaaaaaaaaay worse. Two-year-olds are too young to realize they are aggravating their parents into madness. Logan completely understands what he is doing when he irritates the heck outta me…and he thinks it's hilarious.

Oh, please, can we hurry up and get to his fourth birthday? The year during which a child is three feels like 137 years for a parent. Every day is a battle. It's like his primary mission is to push me to the point where the top of my head blows off.

Nothing is easy with Logan. If I ask him a simple question such as "Do you want some apple juice?" I'll get a multitude of answers including "No. I want milk. Yes. Water. I dunno. Blue Gatorade." How am I supposed to respond to this? I choose the Blue Gatorade, which he promptly slaps out of my hand and spills all over me. Then he yells, "I WANTED APPLE JUICE."

"If you want apple juice, you have to tell me you want apple juice," I respond, as blue liquid drips off the end of my nose.

He starts crying and runs to my wife, "Mommy, Daddy won't give me any apple juice, and he yelled at me." Now, I'm in trouble. He wins. I lose. Game over.

Living with a three-year-old is like coexisting with a very intelligent, highly destructive creature from outer space. He can communicate easily with humans and operate smoothly within our environment. He exploits our love and affection, while he executes his evil plan to demolish everything his mother and I own.

Within a 15-minute time period, Logan can punch a hole in the wall with a Bob the Builder screwdriver, grind graham crackers into the carpet, rub peanut butter all over the couch, whack his brother in the head with a Tonka truck, vomit on his brand new Spiderman shirt, and jam three M&Ms up his nose.

My friends who don't have kids cannot comprehend the magnitude of living with a three-year-old. The other day I saw my friend Brian. "How was your weekend?" I asked.

"It was very relaxing. Sue and I went to a great Italian place for dinner on Friday night. Saturday I played golf, and we had a quiet dinner at the club. Sunday we took a long walk in the park. What did you guys do?"

"Well, my weekend consisted of…stop it, quit it, get off of that counter, stop it, quit throwing toys, stop it, get that Lego out of your nose, stop it, give me the scissors, quit it, ouch, that hurts, leave him alone, stop it, don't throw peas at your brother, stop it, get off your brother's head, stop it, quit it, stop it, I said, STOP IT."

Brian looked at me as if I had seven eyes, two noses, and a home on the planet Klangdar. His mind was trying to process this haphazard collection of data, but it just didn't compute. He'll understand one day when a three-year-old grabs both of his ears, pulls his face into the nose-to-nose position, and screams, "I WANT ICE CREAM…NOW!"

Every activity ends up like a bout in the WWE Toddler Smackdown. My three-year-old will fight over simple things like sitting in his car seat, pushing an elevator button, and sitting in a specific chair at the dinner table. No one is safe, not even the Easter Bunny.

The Saturday before Easter, I told Logan, "The Easter Bunny is coming tonight, and he's going to bring you a basket full of chocolate you can share with Dad!"

"No, it's the Easter Monkey, Daddy," Logan insisted.

"I'm pretty sure he's a bunny, Buddy."

"Nope, it's a monkey dressed up in a bunny suit." At this point, a smart man would have just agreed with him, picked up the TV remote, and found an episode of *Baywatch* (a good one with Pamela Anderson). Not me.

"It's a bunny. I'll prove it. Here, I'll show you a picture of him in the newspaper."

Logan's bottom lip began to quiver. His eyes filled with tears and his face got red. Then his mouth opened wide to release a cry that would signal the beginning of a nuclear meltdown. The mushroom cloud was huge, expanding over five zip codes. I closed my eyes to shield my retinas from the blast. The fallout from this explosion will linger for years.

Chase provided some valuable insight. "Dad, Logan saw a commercial on Cartoon Network with a monkey dressed in a bunny suit. That's why he thinks it's an Easter Monkey."

"Oh. I see. Thanks, son. Don't you think you could have told me that a little sooner?" A wicked grin crossed his face.

The Easter Monkey immediately became a family tradition. Before we went to bed Saturday night, we left three bananas on the dining room table for him. He delivered two heaping baskets of chocolate for the boys, and all was well with the world.

The next week at preschool, Logan told all of his friends about the Easter Monkey. Sadly, the Easter Monkey did not visit their homes. Now, they are all in therapy.

Because Logan was so enamored with the Easter Monkey, I came up with the bright idea to take him to the circus. They'll have lots of monkeys dressed up as clowns riding bicycles and swinging on ropes—the usual monkey antics. He'll love it.

On the day of the circus, Logan was so excited about seeing the monkeys that he was unable to take a nap. WARNING! WARNING! Danger, Will Robinson. We have a three-year-old without a nap. This is a "Code Red Situation."

We arrived at the circus an hour early so we could see a special preshow for kids. Three rings of entertainment were filled with elephants, zebras, tigers, clowns, jugglers…hmmm…no monkeys. Maybe they are temperamental and wait for the real show to come out in front of the crowd. I asked one of the clowns, "Where are the monkeys?"

"We don't have any monkeys."

"What do you mean you don't have any monkeys? This is supposed to be the 'Greatest Show on Earth' so you have to have monkeys. It's a rule."

"Oh, I'm sorry, sir. The rule requires us to have elephants, tigers, and acrobats. Monkeys are optional." *Smartass clown. I am in a buttload of trouble.*

I pulled Starla aside and said, "They don't have any monkeys."

"Didn't you ask about monkeys when you bought the tickets?"

"No, because I am the dumbest man in the universe."

"Daddy, where are the monkeys?" Logan asked. *Here we go.*

"They'll be out soon, Buddy." *Note to self—when you're in a hole, stop digging.*

We took our seats, and the show began with a parade of trapeze artists, contortionists, and clowns. Alligators, llamas, elephants, lions, and tigers strutted around the circus tent.

"Daddy, I don't see any monkeys." Oh no. His bottom lip started quivering.

I tried to change the subject. "Look at the elephants. Do you want some pop-corn? Look at the tigers. Do you want something to drink? Do you have to go to the potty?"

"BWAAAA. I WANNA SEE THE MONKEYS. AAAHHHH." Sniff. Snort. "BWAAAAAAAAAAAA."

I carried Logan out into the lobby, hoping he would wear himself out and fall asleep. Five other dads were in the lobby with similar circumstances. A man car-rying a blubbering three-year-old girl asked me the question of the day: "So, what's your dilemma?"

"No monkeys. How about you?"

"No bears."

Suddenly, Logan stopped crying and said, "What's that?" He pointed to another three-year-old holding a toy with spinning lights. His father looked like he had just won the lottery. Finally, a ray of hope. We found the toy display and purchased a $16.38 hunk of plastic with spinning lights. Life was good. Logan forgot about the monkeys, and we enjoyed the rest of the show...except for that smartass clown. I'd like to run over him with his Lincoln Clown Car.

I envy the three-year-old's unbelievable ability to get what he wants. Logan can make my life a living hell, and I cave in because I need to maintain my sanity. Just once, I'd like to act like a three-year-old in a tense situation.

"Mr. Alderman, my name is Elwood Snodgrass. I'm an auditor with the IRS. Sir, you haven't paid your federal income taxes for the past seven years."

"Yes, I did."

"No...no, sir, you didn't. You haven't filed a tax return in seven years."

"YES...I...DID."

"Mr. Alderman, you are required by federal law to pay your taxes."

"I don't have to...my Mom said."

"She did not. Mr. Alderman, if you don't pay your taxes, I'll have to press charges."

"You will not. You're a weinerhead."

"I'm going to count to three, and you're gonna listen to me, one...two...."

"BWWWWAAAAAAAAAAAA." Sniff. Snort. Deep breath. "AAAAAAAH-HHH."

"All right, fine. Forget the damn taxes! Just please stop crying. What can I do to make you happy?"

"Go to the circus and audit that smartass clown."

Where Does the Money Go?

Some people say, "Money talks." Not my money. Oh noooooo. My money just laughs at me and runs away. Financial experts say it costs an average of more than $170,000 to support a child from birth through the age of 17. This number does not include the cost to replace your ruined carpets, paint your entire house five times, and hire the Lawn Doctor guys to fix the bare spots that have been worn into your yard.

If you're an expectant father, this is how the next few years of your financial life will play out. When you have your first baby, you will buy everything in sight because your wife will tell you to and because you think you might need it. A fancy changing table, special lotions, and expensive clothes will fill your baby's room. Sure, the changing table works great if you're actually in the kid's room, but the rest of the time you'll have to change your kid's diapers in other places like the back seat of your car, the bathroom at Target, or the frozen food section of the Piggly Wiggly. You'll find out the hard way that special lotions make your baby break out in a painful rash, and your kid will outgrow all of his expensive clothes in less than 7.9 seconds. The high-priced merchandise will sit completely unused until your child turns three years old. Then you'll put all of that crap in the basement and swear you'll use it in the future. Here's a shot of reality: you won't.

You will be a much wiser, more experienced parent when your second child arrives. You'll sell your fancy changing table on eBay because you need all the extra cash you can get, and you'll use the same inexpensive baby lotions you smeared on your first kid. If it worked once, it will work again. The second child will wind up wearing every piece of cheap clothing your first child didn't completely destroy. You'll think you've saved a lot of money by raising your second child on a shoestring, but he'll end up costing you big bucks later when you'll drop $120 an hour for his therapy sessions to deal with his low self-esteem issues. You can't win. Don't even try.

When your kids get older, they will move up to high-priced video games, and the cost of their sports equipment will grow exponentially. My kids' sneakers cost more than my shoes, and they grow out of them in three months. I've been wearing the same pair of Reeboks for five years. They smell like the rhinoceros house at the zoo on a hot summer day, but they feel great. Some parents pay more than $100 for their kids' basketball sneakers. If your 12-year-old kid can dunk a basketball and over shoot 66% from behind the three point line, go ahead and buy the expensive shoes. Otherwise, you are wasting your money.

I tried gallantly to save for the boys' college educations. In the late '90s, I amassed a significant chunk of change in their investment funds. I wisely diversified their holdings in growth, income, large cap, small cap, mid cap, foreign, and technology stock mutual funds—a textbook investment strategy. Because I worked for a large management and technology consulting firm, I was very familiar with many of the fast-growth, high-tech firms that were headquartered in Northern Virginia, and I invested in those companies so I could reap the rewards of the dot-com boom. The kids' portfolios held stock in Iridium, PSINet, XO Communications, and many others. Genius, pure genius. I watched with excitement as their portfolios grew every day. I dreamed about what I would do with all of the money I would have left over after they graduated from college.

Then darkness fell upon the planet. The Internet bubble burst, and their mighty portfolios collapsed. My diversification strategy didn't work because every stock classification imploded. The high-tech companies got creamed, and I was too stupid to sell the stock before it became worthless when they filed for bankruptcy. I kept saying, "They'll come back. It's just a matter of time until the stock prices go back up." Oh yeah, and it's just a matter of time until Wyle E. Coyote catches the Road Runner. There's a fine line between being an optimist and being an idiot. I jumped over that line in the spring of 2001.

As I look toward my future expenditures for my kids, one thought keeps popping into my brain: I am so glad I have boys. Don't get me wrong; girls are wonderful and I'm sure they are a blessing to have, but many little girls grow up to be young women who feel the undying desire to have elaborate weddings. Some girls start planning their weddings when they are 12 years old. I feel so sorry for their dads. Who made up the social rule that says the father of the bride is supposed to foot the bill for the wedding? I bet it was a guy who had sons. In any event, I believe this is a sound tradition that should be continued for the foreseeable future or at least until after my boys get married.

Last year, over 2.3 million couples got married. According to *Condé Nast*, the publisher of *Bride's Magazine*, an average wedding in the United States now costs almost $25,000. I'm sure an above-average wedding costs way more. Can you believe that? Dropping 25Gs on a four-hour event seems like a wacky way to dispose of a huge amount of money. Do you realize $25,000 could buy about

100,000 Krispy Kreme donuts? I did the math. I have that kind of time on my hands. I'm not saying that I believe Krispy Kreme donuts are more important than weddings…um…well, let me think about it and I'll get back to you on that one. I just think it's silly to spend that kind of dough for a fleeting moment in time. I know, I know! Marriage is a sacred institution that should be held in the highest regard, blah, blah, blah, but you don't need to spend $3.75 a piece on crab puffs just so you can say, "Congratulations, Herman and Matilda. We hope your marriage lasts longer than these darned crab puffs."

Let's look at an itemized list of a few of the major costs associated with a typical American wedding. Again, these average numbers are provided by *Bride's Magazine*, so they must be true.

- Engagement ring—$3,576. My first car, a 1978 Ford Mustang, cost half that much and lasted longer than many marriages.

- Flowers—$967. Come on, be reasonable here. Flowers wilt and die. Spend your money on something that will last a long time like SPAM. The stuff has a half-life and it comes in a variety of flavors including the traditional SPAM, SPAM Lite, SPAM Smoke Flavored, SPAM Oven Roasted Turkey, and SPAM Less Sodium. It's deeeelicious and contains virtually no carbohydrates!

- Photography and video—$1,814. Many women want to have lovely photographs of their wedding day so they can look back and say, "Wow, I was really skinny back then, but why does my hair look like a bee's nest?" Some people videotape the event. That's fine, just don't force me watch it. I was bored to tears the first time I saw it—please don't put me through that again.

- Wedding favors—$241. Don't give me a candle in a tiny vase or individually wrapped buttermints with an engraved personal message. If you want to do me a favor, change the oil in my car.

- Music—$900. Holy cow! I used to sing at weddings, and I got only a lousy $75. I'm available most weekends. Call me.

- Rehearsal Dinner—$875. I realize I will eventually be the father of the groom, and I'll get stuck with the bill for the rehearsal dinner. Because $875 sounds like a lot of cash for one meal, I'm going to rent a big grill and buy three bags of charcoal. It's burgers and weenies for the entire wedding party.

- Bride's wedding dress—$799, headpiece—$181. That's a lot of money for a dress your daughter will wear only one day. After the wedding, she'll have it sealed away in a box that will sit in the back of her closet for the rest of her life. Think about that when you write a big fat check to Bernie's Bridal Shop.

- Groom's rented formal wear—$100. Just goes to show you the difference between women and men. A woman will spend $1,000 to get a unique wedding dress that fits her perfectly. A man will spend $100 to wear a tuxedo that another guy may have slept in…or worse.

- Wedding reception—$7,630. That's a lotta coin to shell out for a second-rate party. At wedding receptions, I always seem to get stuck sitting at a table with the bride's Great Uncle Clyde and Not-So-Great Aunt Beatrice from Eastern Monmouth, New Jersey. They complain steadily for two hours about how far they had to drive to get to the wedding and how cold it is in their hotel room. There's not enough beer in the world to make that a fun experience.

- Honeymoon—$3,200. Some parents send their daughter and her new hubby off on a grand honeymoon to fantastic locales like Hawaii or the Caribbean. In essence, they pay huge amounts of money for the happy couple to fly long distances so they can spend eight days and seven nights having sex in their hotel room. Let's face it; they could have the same amount of fun in the Holiday Inn in Bluefield, West Virginia, and it costs only $79 a night.

In just a few short years, Chase will meet the girl of his dreams. He'll save his money and buy her a stunning engagement ring. On a special night at dinner, he'll fumble for the right words and say, "I have a very important question to ask you. Will…uh…will you…will you marry me?"

His beautiful girlfriend will throw her arms around him and say, "Oh yes, I'll marry you. Let's start planning our wedding right now."

"OK! Hey, I've got a great idea. Do you like Krispy Kreme donuts?"

Daddy, Are You Awake?

Before the kids came along, I could fall asleep in a nanosecond and easily enjoy nine straight hours of peaceful rest. My Sealy Posturepedic sanctuary provided me with serene dreams of gliding effortlessly over beautiful mountain ranges, sitting quietly in the woods listening to birds singing sweet songs of nature, and watching the annual *Victoria's Secret Lingerie Show* on a big screen TV with no commercial interruptions.

Now, I sleep like a baby. No, I don't mean I snooze in calm tranquility like an infant. I mean my sleep patterns are consistent with those of a baby. I wake up every two hours with pangs of hunger, and then I have to pee.

It all started when Chase was a newborn. I was overly concerned about him and felt the impulse to check on him constantly while he was sleeping. I would wake up in the middle of the night just to see if his breathing was consistent, then I would eat a piece of chocolate pie. Hey, I see no sense in wasting an opportunity to scarf down some chocolate. My obsession with his well-being triggered the onset of my sleep disorder, and the pie triggered the expansion of my big whoppin' belly.

As Chase got older, he amplified my problem. One night when he was about three years old, I was nestled all warm in my bed while visions of Michele Pfeiffer in her vinyl Catwoman bodysuit danced in my head. At approximately 3:26 AM, Chase started screaming at the top of his lungs, "DADDY, HELP ME! I NEED YOU, DADDY!"

A double shot of adrenaline bounced me out of bed. I ran to Chase's room in a panic. Was someone trying to abduct him? Was he in pain? A multitude of scenarios ran through my head as I stumbled down the hall to his room. I burst through his door and found him sitting on the floor beside his bed, crying hysterically.

"What's wrong?"

"I can't find my police car," he sobbed.

"You've got to be kidding me."

"It's dark in here, and I can't see my new police car. I need it right now."

"Chase, it's 3:30 in the morning. Go back to bed. We'll find your police car in the morning when the sun is shining." *Oh yeah, like logic is gonna work on a three-year-old in the middle of the night.*

"Nooooooooooo. I have to find it right now." He burst into tears again and latched on to my leg like a barnacle attached to the bottom of a boat. For the next 30 minutes, we searched for that blasted police car and finally found it under a heap of Lincoln Logs. He climbed into his bed clutching the toy, and I grumbled my way back down the hall.

Forty–five minutes later, right smack in the middle of a good Swedish Bikini Team dream, a strange man's voice cut through the night like a meat cleaver. "Put your hands up." Another flash of adrenaline blew through my veins. I jumped out of bed and assumed the standard "please don't shoot me 'cause I'm a chicken" position. A siren sliced the darkness. The strange voice said, "This is the police. Stop in the name of the law." Standing beside the bed in my underwear with my hands up in the air, I looked over at Starla who hadn't move a muscle throughout the entire ordeal.

"I think Chase is playing with his police car," I said.

"You have an astonishing grasp of the obvious," she murmured.

"I bet I look really stupid right now," I said with my hands still airborne.

"Yep." She laughed at me and rolled over. I went back to Chase's room and discovered him fast asleep under the covers hugging his police car. He had punched a bunch of buttons on the toy in his sleep and slept though the racket. I slowly maneuvered the police car out of his arms and placed it a safe distance away from him.

After a trip to the kitchen for a peanut butter cookie and a pit stop in the bathroom, I crawled back into bed and went back to sleep. This time I dreamed I was being hunted by a drunken banana wearing a policeman's uniform. He was leading a pack of crazed lunatics including a deranged monkey wearing a sombrero, a renegade watermelon with four arms, and Geraldo Rivera. They chased me through a thick wooded area where a chipmunk named Irving tripped me and I fell into a deep hole. The banana started poking me in the eye with a stick. It hurt so badly, I woke up. When I opened my eyes, Chase was poking me in the eye with his finger.

"Daddy, are you awake?"

"I am now. What's the matter?"

"There's a cat in my room."

"We don't have a cat."

"I know, but there's a cat in my room. Can you make it go away?" We traipsed back down the hall to rid his room of the despicable cat that was lurking in the shadows.

Chase pointed to a black lump in the far corner of his room. "There it is," he said as his voice trembled. I walked cautiously to the sinister black lump and kicked it with my foot. At 4:52 AM, I successfully saved my son from the wicked clutches of a Thomas the Train tee shirt.

As I tucked him snugly under his blankets, he asked, "Daddy, is anything hiding under my bed?"

I checked for him. "Nope. Nothing is hiding under your bed."

"But what if I have bad dreams about big scary monsters? They might try to chew my nose off. What will I do, Daddy?"

"You just call me, and I'll come rescue you, Buddy. I'll protect you from any monster that tries to get you…unless it's a banana in a policeman's uniform. Then you're on your own."

Vacations Will
Never Be the Same

Back in the olden days (read: before we had kids), Starla and I took great vacations. We would throw a few bathing suits, tee shirts, and shorts into our small travel bags, and within 20 minutes we were on our way to the beach. For hours, we would lie peacefully on the sand, read, take naps, goof around in the water, and lunch leisurely in the sun. Oh, how I loved to watch the waves crash on the shore, the seagulls glide effortlessly over the water, and the hot young women in minuscule bikinis reject middle-aged men who have thick fur on their backs and think they look good in Speedos that accentuate their enormous, bulging...beer guts.

Vacations are relaxing getaways that help you decompress and forget about the grind of your everyday life. Unfortunately, when you have children, your wonderful vacations transform into trips. Here is the definition of a trip: a family journey that gives your children the opportunity to turn you into a frenzied lunatic at the special rate of $149 a night plus tax and tips.

A few years ago, we made the stupid decision to drive the boys to Myrtle Beach, South Carolina, for a fun-filled family trip. Chase was four years old and Logan had just turned one year old. To prepare for an eight-hour drive and a seven-day excursion with two small kids, Starla packed the car with over six tons of supplies. You name it; she packed it: diapers, wipes, baby clothes, toys, vats of sunscreen, pallets of baby food, crackers, strollers, baby backpacks. As she loaded the provisions into the car, she looked as if she was filling the belly of a 747 with luggage. It took her four hours to jam everything we own into the cargo hold. I walked around to the back of the car with my one undersized duffle bag and asked what I thought was a reasonable question.

"Starla, where do you want me to put my bag?"

"Do you really want me to tell you where you can put your bag?" she replied. Geez, just four hours into our trip and she was already a bit...um, how do I say this...on edge. "There's no room in the back of the car for your bag. You'll have to hold it on your lap."

"But I have to drive the car."

"Yeah…so…what's your point?"

Something told me this was going to be a looooooooong painful car ride, and I may not complete the trip with all of my body parts intact.

Chase squeezed into his booster seat, and I strapped Logan into his child seat. As the driving rule states: children that weigh 20 pounds and under must ride with their child seat facing backwards. I completely agreed with the rule and understood the importance of this safety precaution; however, a critical thought occurred to me.

"Starla, do you think Logan will get carsick if he rides facing backwards? Maybe we should turn him around so he can see where he's going."

"He weighs 20 pounds and the rule says he is supposed to face backwards."

"Ok. Whatever you say is fine with me. I just think it's a bad idea. That's all I'm saying," I responded nervously. She looked like she was going to shove a jar of strained carrots down my throat. Sensing I was in mortal danger, I said, "I know…shut up and drive." I sat my duffle bag on my lap and backed out of the driveway.

Exactly 22 minutes into our eight-hour drive, Logan blew chunks. This was not your every day, run-of-the-mill barf. Oooooh noooooo, this was a cataclysmic "oh crap, we're gonna have to sell the car" type of eruption. He totaled the entire back seat, the floor mats, his car seat, an L.L.Bean bag full of diapers, a complete set of Fantastic Four action figures, and his brother. We had to bury his clothes in a hole by the side of the road. It took us three hours to vacuum out the back seat and salvage the uncontaminated supplies. Needless to say, I turned Logan's car seat around so he could face forward.

As we pulled back on to the road to resume our arduous drive, I looked at Starla in preparation to say, "I told you so." Her ESP kicked in and she gave me the hairy eyeball of death. I smiled sheepishly and said, "I know…shut up and drive."

After traveling all day with the back seat reeking of baby yak and making 57 pee break and diaper change stops along the way, we finally arrived at our hotel in Myrtle Beach. Our eight-hour drive had taken 14 hours to complete. By 8:30 PM, we were all in bed asleep.

The next day at 5:00 AM, Chase poked me in the nose to wake me up and pleaded, "Can we go to the beach now?"

"Sure. Wake up your mom and tell her you want to go to the beach." I turned over and went back to sleep because I knew it would take at least three hours for her to get ready to go. She stuffed two beach bags with four changes of clothes for each boy, loads of snacks and juice boxes, heavy duty beach towels, a first aid kit, and beach toys. Then she lathered the boys with Water Babies Sunscreen with SPF 9,673,826,762 + Aloe, fed them breakfast, and took a shower. At 8:30 AM, I got up, went to the bathroom, and put on my bathing suit. With only five minutes of prep time, I was ready to go to the beach to have some fun in the sun.

I felt like a pack mule as I toted the heavy bags to the beach. We slogged through the sand to find the perfect spot—close to the water, no rocks or shells, and just 10 feet away from two college girls wearing string bikinis. As Starla unpacked our beach paraphernalia, I grabbed a Nerf football and began playing catch with Chase and Logan.

Ten minutes into our beach football game, Chase said, "Dad, the sand is really hot. Can we go to the pool?"

"No, we just got here. Come on; let's have some fun in the sand." I threw a pass to Logan, and he tumbled into the surf. He got wet sand in his swim diaper and began to cry because he had a big hunk of sand stuck to his butt. The ocean winds blew sand into Chase's eyes and he began crying. We were so loud and annoying that the college girls got up and left. The day was not working out the way I had planned.

I caved. "All right, let's go to the pool." We moved to the hotel pool, and the boys played vigorously in the water until they were completely exhausted. By 11:00 AM, we had returned to our hotel room, eaten lunch, and put the boys down for their midday naps. Starla read a novel, and I watched *The Price Is Right*. What happened to our fun in the sun? The boys woke up at 3:00 PM so we took them out for a round of miniature golf and dinner at McDonald's.

Our evening consisted of 15 episodes of "stop jumping on the bed and yelling because there are people in the next room," five occurrences of "no we can't go home now because we're eight hours from home and we're on VACATION," and two bath fights. By 9:00 PM, the kids were asleep and I was bored. Couldn't watch TV because it would wake the kids. Couldn't eat because their food radar would go off and I would be forced to share my Little Debbie Snack Cakes with the boys. I went to sleep dreaming that I was lying on a secluded Caribbean beach surrounded by crystal blue water, beautiful pure white sand, and 42 boxes of Little Debbie Snack Cakes.

We spent the next five days swimming in the hotel pool, going to IMAX movies, playing countless rounds of miniature golf, strolling down Myrtle Beach's grand strand, and shopping for tee shirts in souvenir shops. The boys had fun, and it turned out to be a pretty good trip after all. On the last day of our journey, as we were getting into the car to go home, I said, "I can't believe we traveled for hundreds of miles to do things we could have done at home. Over the entire week, we spent less than 30 minutes on the beach."

Starla just stared at me. A cold chill of fright sprinted down my spine. I started the engine and said, "I know…shut up and drive."

SuperChildren of the Corn

Every parent wants his or her kid to be smart and successful, but have you noticed how some parents become obsessed with increasing the intelligence or athletic abilities of their young children to staggering levels? Don't get me wrong; I absolutely agree with encouraging kids to learn and pursue goals, but drilling a five-year-old on the complexities of the Pythagorean Theorem seems a bit excessive.

I believe these pushy parents are trying to make up for their failures in life. They didn't get into Harvard or win an Olympic gold medal in swimming, so they try to salvage their shattered dreams by living vicariously through their children. Maybe they're dreadfully insecure or they have some sort of success complex. Whatever the reason, these people place unnecessary pressure on their kids to overachieve. The strain of constant training builds anxiety and can send a child into a deep depression. If you are one of these parents, LIGHTEN UP. You don't want your nine-year-old kid to run away from home, sleep on a street corner, and spend his days trying to score a pack of M&Ms.

It starts with the birth of the golden child. Fanatical parents immediately begin to compare their baby to other newborns. They say things like, "My little Johnny's head circumference is in the 95th percentile. His brain is far larger than everyone else's; therefore, he is certain to be a genius." These zealots act like raising a child is some sort of competition. They prattle on incessantly about how their precious Johnny turned over on his belly before anyone else his age; how he started walking at seven months; and how while other children's' first words are usually "Dada" and "Mama," precious Johnny's first words were "maternal caregiver." Persistent parental demands over the next 18 years drive Johnny into the comforting confines of his parents' basement where he smokes joints, eats HoHos, drinks orange soda, and watches *Jeopardy* every day. Yeah, Johnny can answer every question Alex Trebek throws out, but he can't hold a conversation with another human being. I'm guessing this is not exactly the outcome his mom and dad had in mind.

The other day at Logan's pre-school, I saw Julie Kiplinger, one of these rabid, overachieving parents. Every time I see Julie, she blathers on about her geeky four-year-old Jamie's latest accomplishment.

"You'll never guess what book Jamie just finished. Go ahead and tell Logan's daddy the name of the book you finished reading last night, Jamie."

Jamie self-consciously said, "The name of the book is *The Da Vinci Code*. It's an interesting examination of the world's greatest mysteries. I found it to be quite exhilarating." Can you believe this? At only four years old, this kid is reading a best seller and using the words "quite exhilarating" correctly in a sentence. That's eerie.

My male competitive gene kicked into high gear. Although he hasn't started reading yet, Logan is a very smart kid. I poked Logan in the shoulder and said, "Tell Jamie's mom the name of the book we read together last night."

Logan looked up at Jamie's mom and said, "My daddy has a black mushnash on his lip."

"Ha! Oh boy, isn't that funny? He can't say moustache yet, so he calls it a mushnash. Now, come on Logan, tell Mrs. Kiplinger the name of the book we read last night. Remember…it was about a train…Thomas the Train."

"My daddy picks his nose in the car."

"Oh geez, would you look at the time. We'd better get home. Logan, tell Jamie bye." We scrambled off into our car, and I drove away as fast as I could to escape the humiliation.

What kind of nutty parent has her four-year-old reading books like *The Da Vinci Code*? She's going to drive Jamie straight to Wackyville by pushing him so hard. Who knows what this kid will be like by the time he turns 10 years old? He'll probably become the leader of a pack of SuperChildren who will construct a secret headquarters in a secluded Nebraska cornfield and devise a plot to rule the world.

The SuperChildren will use their enormous brains to orchestrate a hostile takeover of CEC Entertainment, the owner of hundreds of Chuck E. Cheese restaurants. Jamie will direct his legion of ultraintelligent children to use their highly evolved computer skills to reprogram the video games in the restaurants and to broadcast subliminal messages to normal children. The messages will repeatedly tell the kids how to access their parents' bank accounts and wire all of their money to a numbered Swiss bank account. After the league of extraordinary children collects billions of dollars through this diabolical scheme, they'll use the money to buy the entire state of Oregon and turn it into a gigantic amusement park. They'll build huge Marriott Residence Inns and allow kids to live in freedom without any parental pressure. No anxiety, no differential equations, no Latin, no science projects, no swim team practice at 5:00 AM, no overbearing gymnastics coaches, no fanatical soccer parents. The place will be a kiddie Utopia. Their marketing slogan will be "Oregon—Where a Kid Can Be a Kid!"

Their sinister plan will culminate in a final act of youthful unity. The SuperChildren will harness the collective strength of millions of youngsters from all over the world to invade and occupy the state of California, where every kid will run for governor.

As you raise your children, think about the damage you could do to their mental stability by shoving them toward hollow achievements. Let your children live their own lives. They may be wildly successful or they may not. In either event, they need to develop at their own individual pace. Don't obsess so much about the progression of their learning curve. Don't become an accomplishment addict. And for Pete's sake, don't let your kid tell anyone that you pick your nose in the car.

The Farmer Cuts the Cheese

A few years ago, my company conducted an executive conference at a luxury hotel in Charleston, South Carolina. The term "executive conference" actually means a three-day escape for management on the company's nickel. We held meetings for a couple of hours each morning and then participated in team building activities every afternoon. By team building activities, I mean golf, tennis, massages, and general goofing off.

Because I was a highly devoted executive, I demonstrated my dedication to the firm by taking my family with me on the boondoggle. I also scored major points with Starla because she adores Charleston. On the first day of the conference, while I attended the initial morning meetings, Starla and the kids toured Charleston's Historic District. We met for lunch at our favorite restaurant, Poogan's Porch, and planned our afternoon team-building activities.

After lunch, we headed out on a mission to tour the Battery, a famous row of gorgeous homes lining the Charleston peninsula. Ten minutes into our mission, I spied my boss, Antonio Walken, with his family on the other side of the street. He waved for us to come over and meet his wife, Maria, and daughters Jennifer and Chantal. I tried to suck up to Antonio by urging my oldest son, Chase, to shake his hand and formally introduce himself. At the time, Chase was four years old and very precocious.

"Go ahead. Shake Mr. Walken's hand, Buddy," I coached.

Chase took Antonio's hand and said, "Nice to meet ya, Mr. Walken. My dad says you're a loser…loser, loser, loser." He repeated the word loser approximately 872 times while I tried to explain my way out of the deep hole my son had dug for me. I learned a very valuable lesson that day: Antonio does not have a sense of humor.

Both of my kids have a remarkable ability to remember and repeat the worst phrases that come out of my mouth. One day I was playing with Logan. We were having a blast making up new lyrics to the kid's song "The Farmer in the Dell." I came up with the line "the farmer cuts the cheese," which Logan thought was the funniest thing he had ever heard. For three months, he sang that line in school, church, Sears, the doctor's office, and every public forum he could find. The other dads who heard him thought it was hilarious. Other moms just stared at me in revulsion because Logan taught it to their kids.

Logan also combines his musical talent with an innate sense of timing. A few weeks ago, Starla took him grocery shopping. She plopped him into the grocery cart child seat and worked her way through the aisles. Because Logan was squarely in the middle of his *Shrek* phase (he had watched the video twice a day for three weeks), he decided to sing songs from the movie as his mom filled the cart. As they meandered through the frozen food section, they passed a lady with…um…a rather large caboose. She was packin' a lot of junk in the trunk if ya know what I'm sayin'. At the top of his lungs, Logan started singing his favorite song from *Shrek*: "I like BIG BUTTS and I cannot lie." The lady was the store manager. We don't shop there anymore.

Chase has not yet learned the concept of "tell Mom only what she needs to know." One day I was in the living room, reading a fascinating series of poems by Emily Dickenson…well, no, that's not true…actually I was watching an episode of *Leave it to Beaver,* and the Beav was reading the poems for a school project. It's the same thing.

I overheard Chase talking to Starla in the kitchen. "Hey, Mom…great hooters," he blurted without considering the consequences of his actions.

"Where did you hear that?" she asked. *I have the right to remain silent. Anything he says can and will be held against me for the next 50 years.*

"Dad said it when he saw a girl at the mall this morning." *Dead man walkin'.* I had three potential responses available:

1. He's lying. *No, you can't call your kid a liar. That's bad.*

2. He's confused. *No, you can't call your kid stupid. That's also bad.*

3. I'm going to my room so I can think about what I did wrong. *Bingo.*

This incident cost me a gold tennis bracelet, an evening at the ballet, and two weeks of *Trading Spaces* reruns. It could have been worse. She could have made me watch *Mr. Personality.* After the incident blew over, I had a man-to-man talk with Chase.

"Look, Chase, you don't need to tell Mom everything I do. Some things should stay between us. You know…guy things."

"Like when you steal Mom's *Victoria's Secret* catalog?"

"Yes, that's a good example."

"And telling Mom you have to run an errand but you really go to Chick-fil-A?"

"Yes, you've got the idea. Let's move on."

"And when you wear her clothes?"

"I did that one time as a joke...and I looked pretty good. Now, are we clear?"

"Yes, Dad. But I have one more question. What are hooters?"

Happy Father's Day

Contrary to popular opinion, Father's Day was not created by greeting card companies to expand their product lines. Historians who had way too much time on their hands traced the origin of Father's Day to a woman named Sonora Louise Smart Dodd, who initiated the observance of the holiday. Because there was already a day established to honor mothers, Sonora believed there should be time set aside to show respect for fathers. So on June 19, 1910, Sonora gave her dear old dad a year's subscription to *Fishing Digest,* and Father's Day was born.

Although Sonora worked diligently to promote her idea, Father's Day never became a Tier One holiday like Mother's Day, Independence Day, Thanksgiving, or Memorial Day. Heck, it isn't even considered to be in the same league with the Tier Two holidays such as Columbus Day, Arbor Day, and President's Day. Father's Day languishes in irrelevance with other mediocre Tier Three holidays including these:

- Old Rock Day, January 7. I'm not sure what ceremony is used to observe Old Rock Day, but I'm pretty sure it includes a tribute to Keith Richards.

- National Dress Up Your Pet Day, January 14. Can you imagine how embarrassing it must be for a German shepherd to be seen in public wearing a pair of lederhosen?

- National Multiple Personalities Day, March 5. I love this holiday, and so do I.

- National Pigs in a Blanket Day, April 24. Every year I cry because those little piggies are so adorable in their tiny blankets. They are so cute. I could just eat 'em up.

- Lumpy Rug Day, May 3. I can't tell if this is a day to commemorate old floor coverings or bad toupees worn by fat guys named Louie and Sid.

- National Nude Day, July 14. Caution: if you attend a National Nude Day barbeque, STAY AWAY FROM THE GRILL.

- National Fight Procrastination Day, September 6. This holiday has been rescheduled to October 17.

Father's Day will never be in the same league as Mother's Day. Throughout the country, mothers are pampered, indulged, and honored on their special day. Elaborate Mother's Day brunches are filled with families who feel compelled to say "thanks" to the women who loved them and cared for them for so many years. For Father's Day, Dad has to drive the whole family to IHOP, and then he gets stuck with the bill for seven rooty tooty fresh and fruity breakfasts and an apple crisp dessert for old lardbutt, Aunt LuWanda.

Telecommunications companies report that Mother's Day is the peak day of the year for long distance telephone calls. In contrast, more collect calls are recorded on Father's Day than on any other day of the year. Father's Day collect calls usually sound like this:

Operator: "Collect call from Eugene in St. Louis. Will you accept the charges?"

Dad: "Hurrumph."

Operator: "I'll take that as a 'Yes.' You're connected."

Eugene: "Hi, Dad, this is Eugene. Happy Father's Day!"

Dad: "The Weather Channel says it's gonna rain today. Is it raining there in St. Louis?"

Eugene: "No, but it's kinda cloudy."

Dad: "We need the rain. I hope it rains today." Awkward extended silence.

Eugene: "So…is Mom there?"

On Mother's Day, moms are showered with expensive, meaningful presents like jewelry and flowers. Father's Day presents have evolved from the traditional repulsive, unwearable tie to a hoard of gadgets that Dad will never use. Just walk though any department store on the Saturday before Father's Day, and you'll see ridiculous inventions like the computer keyboard vacuum. Look, I don't vacuum the floor of my home. Do you really think I'm gonna take time to suck the chocolate chip cookie crumbs out of my computer keyboard? I know the crumbs are about to ruin the squiggly line key (the one that looks like this ~), but I never use the darn thing and I don't care what happens to it.

Some Father's Day devices are just plain silly. Who the heck needs a battery-operated shoe shine kit? Shining your shoes isn't what you would call a physically challenging activity for those few guys who actually shine their shoes. I doubt this high-tech contraption would have any substantial effect on my ratty old Reeboks, so please don't buy one for me.

A few Father's Day gift concepts attempt to smash many items into one all-purpose doohickey that Dad will put in the garage, ignore for 20 years, and eventually throw away when he retires to Sun City, Arizona. A prime example is the combination flashlight, radio, television, MP3 player, hibachi grill, nail clipper, and weed whacker that is displayed in stores only during the week before Father's Day because no people in their right mind would buy it for any other occasion.

Families need to be sensitive to the fact that some Father's Day gifts remind Dad of his advancing age. Although a family may have the best intentions in mind, giving Dad an electric nose hair trimmer for Father's Day actually says to him, "We love you Daddy, but you're getting older, and it looks as if you have a gray squirrel up your nose." When I was younger, I never had a nose hair crisis, but now it's completely out of control. Since I turned 40, I have found thickets of gray hair sticking out of my nose and growing on the outside of my ears. My eyebrows look like geriatric caterpillars. Pretty soon my whole head will be covered with coarse gray wool, and I'll look like an old sheep. [Insert your favorite sheep joke here.]

Pre-school age kids love to make gifts for their dads for Father's Day. When Chase was four years old, he supposedly worked for a week to design a special treat just for me. At 6:02 AM on Father's Day, he woke me up by dropping a small paper bag on my face.

"Happy Father's Day, Daddy! I made a present for you," he exclaimed with excitement. I opened the bag to find a brown oblong rock with two black globs of paint on one end and a green pipe cleaner taped to the other end.

"Thank you, Chase. What is it?"

"It's a rock mouse."

"Oh, yes. Of course, it's a rock mouse."

"You can put it in your office next to your computer."

He was so proud of his creation and I didn't want to disappoint him, so I put the poor excuse for a mouse on my desk. Everyone who came into my office asked me, "Why do you have a rock on your desk?" Every time I responded with the same answer, "For your information, it's a mouse...and my son made it for me."

After two weeks of getting razzed about my rock mouse from the entire population of the ninth floor, including the lady who waters the plants, I made an executive decision to rub out the mouse. I carried him to an out-of-the-way trash can and buried him under a stack of discarded PowerPoint presentations.

The next day, without warning me in advance, Starla brought Chase by my office to surprise me and take me out to lunch. As soon as Chase walked in, he asked, "Where's my rock mouse, Daddy?" Busted.

I tried to think fast on my feet and said, "It's a sad story, Buddy. A rock cat got loose in the office and ate the rock mouse. I'm so sorry."

"Was it really gross?" he asked, obviously quite concerned about his creation.

"Yes, it took me three hours to clean up the mess."

"Cool." His eyes sparkled with intrigue. Four-year-old boys will buy any story if it involves something gross. The next year, he made me another rock mouse because I liked the first one so much. It's still sitting on my desk.

Greeting cards are often given to express a child's feeling for his or her parents. Mother's Day cards convey feelings of love and respect toward that special woman in your life who will always be your biggest fan. Usually, Mother's Day cards say something sincere such as the following:

> *How fortunate I am to have a mother like you. I will always remember your warm hugs, your caring smile, and your sweet voice telling me everything would be all right. You have touched my life in every way—what a beautiful gift from a wonderful woman. I love you, Mom. Happy Mother's Day.*

Father's Day cards don't communicate the same expression of heartfelt affection. Oh sure, children love their dads, but they don't get mushy with elaborate demonstrative prose. Typically, Father's Day cards are short and to the point like this:

> *Dad, you always wanted the best for me.*
> *You sacrificed much, I suppose.*
> *But today I must shout, it really creeps me out*
> *To see that gray squirrel up your nose.*

Don't Hit Your
Brother With a Stick

There are some phrases you don't normally hear in daily conversation, such as these: "Yo, Bob, could you hand me that cement mixer?" "I wish the federal government would raise my taxes." Or "Honey, for our anniversary, I'm taking you to Hooters." Normal human beings don't use absurd expressions like these, unless they are parents of young children.

Since I became a dad, I constantly catch myself making ridiculous statements that pop out of my mouth without warning. Taken out of context, these statements would surely qualify me for a white jacket with long arms that tie in the back and for a padded room in an institution. To keep the boys from obliterating our house and each other, I have to dole out obscure instructions that make me sound like a doofus. Here are some examples of phrases I have actually used with the boys:

- Get your feet off the wall.

- You can't ride the coffee table like a surfboard.

- Don't hit your brother with a stick.

- Get that pencil out of your ear.

- Spiderman does too take a bath.

- You can't put the dog in the refrigerator.

- The couch is not a trampoline.

- Trust me, eleventeen is not a number.

- Red crayons do not taste like ketchup.

Holding a rational telephone conversation in our home is darned near impossible. The ringing of a phone attracts Logan like a moth to a flame. When Starla is on the phone, Logan seizes the opportunity to distract her to the point where her blood pressure rises to 350 over 275. He forces her to blurt out a string of statements that have no rhyme or reason. A typical phone conversation between Starla and her mother sounds like this:

"Hi, Mom, how are you? Don't drink out of the dog's bowl. No, not you, Mom, I was talking to Logan. I don't know where your left sock is. No, boys cannot fly. Yes, Dad has lots of hair on his back. No, Nana is not going to bring you a pony. Get that crayon out of your nose. Yes, I am wearing underpants. No you cannot see them. Will you please go away? No, I wasn't talking to you, Mom. Mom?"

Arbitrary commands squirt out in public when you least expect them. A couple of years ago, we took the boys to Walt Disney World in Orlando. Chase had just turned five years old and Logan was almost two years old. The park is called the "Happiest Place on Earth." The kids had a blast. Yes, all right, so did I.

After lunch, Starla assigned me the task of watching Logan. She wrangled with him all morning, so now it was my turn to keep him out of trouble. As we tooled around the park, we met many of the famous Disney characters: Mickey, Minnie, Goofy (he looks much taller on television), and Donald Duck. Starla asked Pinocchio where the bathrooms were, and he told us they were in the trees behind Space Mountain. Liar.

We paid a small fortune for a round of ice cream and found a spot on Main Street where we could watch the afternoon parade of Disney Stars. Our favorite cartoon celebrities passed by on huge colorful floats. Hercules, Tigger, and Simba waved to the kids in a glorious celebration of fun, laughter, and retail merchandising.

My favorite float used an aquatic theme with fish, coral, and dolphins surrounding the Little Mermaid, Ariel, a gorgeous redhead with a great set of…uh…seashells. Yeah, let's go with seashells. I was mesmerized by her beauty and the tiny bra she was wearing. I held Logan's hand tightly to keep him safe, but my eyes were on Ariel. Although I could feel Logan moving around, I figured I had him under control, until I heard Starla's voice behind me: "Logan, don't lick the trashcans at Walt Disney World." He snapped to attention, and I quickly returned to the real world from my Little Mermaid daydream. Did she just say what I think she said? Noooooo. That doesn't make any sense. Who in his right mind would lick a trashcan? Logan would.

"I thought you were watching him," Starla said.

"I was watching him…just…not when he was licking the trashcan." Starla washed Logan's mouth out with some liquid stuff she had in her purse. She then explained how dangerous germs live in trashcans and make little boys very sick. Needless to say, this Microbiology 101 lesson was wasted on the headstrong two-year-old.

"Can I lick something else?" he asked.

"No. Don't lick anything else for the rest of your life."

"OK, Mommy," Logan said, as he licked the bottom of his left shoe.

That night in our hotel room, we laughed about the licking incident. Well, actually, come to think of it…I laughed, but Starla didn't seem to find the humor in the incident. The boys went to sleep as soon as their heads hit their pillows. Starla and I sat on the couch, enjoying the sound of silence. "Honey," I whispered softly.

She replied gently, "Yes, I am wearing underpants and, no, you cannot see them."

Strike Three, Strike Four, Strike Five

When I was a kid, I dreamed of playing baseball for the Baltimore Orioles. I desperately wanted to play shortstop beside Brooks Robinson. I loved to hear the crack of the bat, smell the sweet infield grass, and dodge the splatter of spit in the dugout.

My dream almost came true. The only thing that kept me from playing major league baseball was my lack of talent…and I was slow…and I couldn't hit a curveball…and I adjusted my cup a bit too often.

I still have delusions of playing in Camden Yard. I can almost see it: bottom of the ninth inning, two out, bases loaded. We're tied with the Yankees. I walk slowly to the plate, turn to the batboy, and say, "Hey, kid, hold my hot dog and beer. I'll be right back." I dig into the batter's box, take a couple of practice swings, get winded, take a time out, and inhale a few snorts of oxygen. Now, I'm ready to hit.

Just like Babe Ruth, I raise my arm and point—to the dugout. That's probably where I'll be very soon. The Pitcher, Roger "The Rocket" Clemens, throws a fastball traveling at a speed of more than 700 MPH. I look at him and laugh because there ain't no freakin' way I'm gonna hit the heat. Next he throws a curve that breaks approximately 39 feet. Strike two.

"Say, Roger," I yell. "Can I have your autograph? It's for my kids."

"Sure, no problem," he says. Roger is such a nice guy.

I lean over the plate for the third pitch. Roger chucks a fastball, high and inside. The ball wallops me in the side of the head, knocking me unconscious. The runner on third base scores and we win the game. Four hours later, I wake up in the hospital and say, "Where's that darned batboy with my hot dog and beer?" Life as a pro baseball player—it doesn't get any better than that.

Because my career as a professional athlete didn't quite work out the way I had planned, I have transferred the dream to my boys. Like many fathers, when my first son was born, I immediately bought him a baseball glove, bat, hat, jock, bat-

ting helmet, sports attorney, and endorsement agent. You can never be too prepared for athletic greatness.

Unfortunately, I had no idea I would have to wait five years for him to
become remotely interested in baseball. Those were the longest five years of my
life. Finally, the time came to sign Chase up for his first year of baseball in the
Tee Ball League.

I was giddy. "You want to play baseball, right?"

"I dunno."

"Come on, it will be a lot of fun." It's not pretty when a 40-year-old man
whines.

"Will I get a trophy?" he asked.

"Yes," I said, confidently. *Man, I hope they give out trophies.*

The first day of practice, our coach, Sid, asked the dads to work with their kids
on basic skills: throwing, hitting, and fielding. I was in heaven.

I took Chase out to the shortstop position. "OK, when you get a grounder, get
your body in front of the ball. Bend your knees. Get your butt down, glove near
the ground, eye on the ball, catch it on a good hop, and come up throwing
quickly to first base."

"I have to pee."

After a visit to the filthiest porta-potty I have ever seen, we decided to work on
hitting. I prepared the tee. "OK, Chase. It's simple. See the ball. Hit the ball.
Give me a good level swing. All right, here we go."

I was sure Chase would smack the ball with authority. Swing and a miss.
"That's OK. Keep your eye on the ball, Buddy." Another swing and a miss. "Give
it a ride, son." Whiff. Four cuts later, he thumped the middle of the batting tee
and the ball fell off into fair territory. "Way to go! Run to first base!" This was
going to be a long season. We suffered through five more practice sessions in
preparation for our first game.

Game day arrived on a sunny Saturday. Chase looked great in his uniform. I
was thrilled. My boy was officially a baseball player. As we walked to the field,
Starla said, "Don't play too hard."

I blew a gasket. "Don't tell him that! For three weeks I've been BEGGING
him to play hard. Are you outta your mind?"

"He shouldn't get overheated. He had a fever two days ago. Do you want your
son to be sick? I don't think you do, Mister." I put my gasket back on.

Our team took the field first. Trying to place a group of five-year-olds in baseball positions is like herding grasshoppers. As soon as you get one of them in

place, he jumps somewhere else. The kids on our team were…ummm…very active. Let's put it this way, our team should have been sponsored by Ritalin.

Initially, I was afraid Chase was going to be the worst player on the team because he couldn't hit, throw, or field. As it turned out, no one could hit, throw, or field on either team. Dads had to tell their kids when to run and where to throw the ball. Kids were playing in the dirt, turning around backwards to look at airplanes in the sky, and running off the field to catch the Good Humor man.

We took our turn at bat in the bottom of the first inning. I put a batting helmet on Chase's head and gave him some words of encouragement, "It's showtime big guy. Remember, see the ball; then hit the ball. Swing hard and level. Relax your hands. Bend your knees. Turn your hips. Flick your wrists."

"I have to pee."

"You can pee after you hit. Go up to the plate." I placed the ball on the tee and adjusted the height for him. *Oh, please hit the ball.* He took his first swing. Strike one.

"How was that, Dad?"

"You look like your Nana. Swing harder." He took another miserable whack. Strike two. The torture continued. Strike three. Strike four. Strike five. According to Tee Ball regulations, a child can keep trying until the ball is hit into fair territory, or until the completion of the next Presidential election—whichever comes first.

Strike six. I remained positive. "Seventh time is the charm, Buddy."

I don't know what happened to Chase on his next swing. Maybe the baseball gods felt sorry for us and cast a magic spell on his bat. He ripped a line drive into right field. My jaw dropped. He took off, running like a cheetah toward third base. I turned him around and pointed him in the right direction. The other team managed to throw the ball into the parking lot, so he arrived safely at first base.

Chase had a fantastic first game. He punched two more singles, stopped a ground ball with his forehead, and threw a dirt clod over 20 feet. The game ended in a tie, 36 to 36. As Chase sat on the dugout bench and ate his postgame snack of chocolate cookies, I became overwhelmed with emotion, "Son, I love you and I'm so proud of you."

He looked up at me with a cookie-covered grin and said, "I have to pee."

Mine Is Bigger Than Yours

Sibling rivalry has been a fact of life since Cain whacked Abel. Throughout time, siblings have argued over critical issues such as capitalism vs. socialism, Republican vs. Democrat, and great taste vs. less filling.

The contention starts as soon as a sibling arrives on the scene. Chase was three years old when his brother, Logan, was born. When he saw the new baby in the hospital, Chase said, "Hi. I'm your brother, Chase. I'm bigger than you. Stay away from my stuff."

I'm convinced my sons have a competitive gene that can trigger haphazard competitive statements at any point in time. One morning we were eating breakfast. The boys were chomping on cereal, and I was crunching bran (yes, bran; I'm over 40). The competitive gene engaged. Chase fired the first shot.

"My Cheerios are bigger than yours."

Without blinking, Logan said, "I have more milk than you."

"My spoon is bigger."

"I have more Legos than you." The competition turned into a fight. Punches flew in every direction. I got cracked in the nose trying to separate them. They laughed hysterically at me and returned to their chomping.

There is no end in sight. I'm sure they'll squabble their entire lives. Eighty years from now, they'll be sitting on a front porch in rocking chairs, drinking Ensure. Logan, the troublemaker, will start the clash.

"My liver spots are bigger than yours."

"Oh yeah, my prostate is bigger than yours."

"Well, my [censored] is bigger than yours."

"How do you know? You haven't used your [censored] in 30 years."

"You're an old fart." They laugh hysterically, have another Ensure, and proceed with a contest to see who can break the most wind in 30 minutes.

Let's face it; farts are hilarious. Oh sure, women think they're disgusting, but virtually every man thinks farts are the funniest things on the planet. Don't believe me? Ask any guy to describe the movie *Blazing Saddles*. The first thing he mentions will be the famous campfire scene where a bunch of cowboys eat supper and rip farts that would make your grandma gag. Now that's funny.

Chase critiques movies by their strategic use of flatulence in a script. *Treasure Planet* includes a character that communicates by farting—this movie received three toots on a scale of five potential toots. *Dr. Doolittle 2* featured a bear that farts. This film garnered five toots for innovative use of gas by an animal. Very impressive. The first *Scooby Doo* movie featured Scooby and Shaggy in a no-holds-barred farting competition. Every time Chase watches that scene, he laughs his head off. So do I.

Many other movies could have benefited from the tactical use of farts. Because *Titanic* was such a long movie (approximately 483 hours), it could have been spiced up with a good fart in the right place: "I'm king of the fffffrrrrrttt." *Casablanca* would have been revered as a classic comedy if Humphrey Bogart had said, "Play it again, fffffrrrrrttt." And of course, in *Gone With The Wind*, Rhett Butler should have said, "Frankly my dear, I don't give a fffffrrrrrttt."

Everyone farts, but in different ways. The Queen of England probably has someone to fart for her. After dinner, she probably calls out to her manservant, "Jeeves, please send for the Royal Farter immediately. I am in desperate need of an invigorating fish and chips fart."

All musicians fart. Evidently, Michael Jackson farts a lot because his kids are always wearing those dopey masks. Every time Sean Combs farts, he gets a new nickname. That's how he originally got the name, Puff Daddy. Justin Timberlake's farts play the song "Bye, Bye, Bye." Some people believe Elvis farts are still alive.

Beautiful people fart. I bet when Cindy Crawford farts, it smells like a bouquet of roses. Famous people fart. When Donald Rumsfeld farts, a smart bomb is automatically launched at an Al Qaeda hideout in Afghanistan. Even infamous people fart. When OJ Simpson farts, he pleads not guilty and vows to find the "real" farter.

I wish farts could become more acceptable in society. Wouldn't it be great if Tom Brokaw started a news broadcast with, "Good evening. I'm Tom Brokaw with NBC News. Today in Washington D.C., the Senate debated a new fffffrrrrrttt tax cut."

Or imagine you are in a receiving line at the White House preparing to meet the President and the First Lady. You feel a big one welling up. You finally make your way to the First Lady, "Ma'am, it is a great honor to fffffrrrrrttt meet you." I am certain she would be horribly offended. I am also certain the President (being a guy and all) would laugh so hard that champagne would come out of his nose. He would tell that story for the rest of his life and laugh until he cried every time.

On the next episode of *American Idol*, I would love to see Ruben Studdard and his brother Kevin sing "Anything You Can Do, I Can Do Better" while conducting a farting contest. Kevin, who is approximately the size of Montana, would cut a slice of cheese big enough to blow spindly Clay Aiken into another network. Ruben has the potential to release enough natural gas to heat every home in New Jersey for an entire winter. Safety note: Under no circumstances should you ever pull Ruben's finger. These flatulent giants could propel sibling competition to the highest level possible. The *American Idol* judges would weigh in with their esteemed opinions:

Randy Jackson: "Yo, Yo, Yo. 'Sup, dawgs? It was off the hook." *What the heck did he say?*

Paula Abdul: "Ruben, I love the you that is you, and you are the you that you know you are. Great job." *I don't care if she rambles incoherently. Paula is hot.*

Simon Cowell: "Ruben, you were good, but Kevin's toot had more quality."

Ruben would just smile and say, "I don't care because mine was bigger."

Business Travel Sucks

As I'm writing this chapter, I'm sitting on an airplane at Dulles Airport. Just sitting—not flying. For four freakin' hours, we have been parked on the runway, waiting for the air traffic control center to give us clearance to take off. Apparently, severe thunderstorms at Chicago's O'Hare Airport have shut down all air traffic in the surrounding area. We can't go back to the terminal because we would lose our place in line, so we're trapped in this plane with a lousy air conditioning system on the hottest day ever recorded in the history of mankind. This is great. Just great.

A tall, dark-haired guy sitting in the window seat of my row thought it would be a good idea to go to the gym and work out before the flight. He could find a way to crunch through 200 sit-ups, but just couldn't bring himself to take a shower before he got on the plane. Now the entire aircraft smells like an old sneaker filled with rotten broccoli. Jackass.

An overweight man in a bad Sears suit is sitting in the middle seat next to me. His Burger King–laden butt is squeezed into his chair, and my Chick-fil-A–enhanced belly is wedged between the arms of my aisle seat. Man, it's so hot that we are sweating like two pigs at a pork pullin' barbeque. We're sweating like Anna Nicole Smith taking a physics test. We're sweating like Bill Clinton judging the Miss Razorback Beauty Pageant at the Little Rock State Fair. You get the idea.

Sitting directly behind me is an engaged couple, Todd and Danielle. They have been at each other's throats since they checked in at the gate. It seems her father thinks Todd is an idiot because he dropped out of Georgetown's law program to pursue a career as a political cartoonist. Todd's mother thinks Danielle is a spoiled rich girl because she made Todd buy her a $6,000 engagement ring he couldn't afford. For the last four hours, they have fought about where they were going to live, how many children they were going to have, and how often they were going to have sex every week. Todd lobbied to have sex four times a week, which made me burst into uncontrollable laughter. Danielle told Todd if he didn't shut up, he would be lucky if he ever had sex again.

Dylan, the three-year-old sitting in front of me, is the Red Power Ranger. I know this because he has told me 3,437 times since we boarded the plane. I am very familiar with this secret superhero organization because my son, Logan, is the Blue Power Ranger. They both probably work out of the Washington, D.C. Power Ranger field office.

I'm beyond bored. I've already finished the Dean Koontz novel I brought with me, and I've read the in-flight magazine three times. What can I do now? I know, I'll call Starla to let her know my flight was delayed.

"Hi, it's me."

"Are you in Chicago?"

"No, we're sitting on the airplane at Dulles Airport. We can't take off because thunderstorms have forced the FAA to close O'Hare Airport. We have to wait until the storms move out of the Chicago area."

"Bummer. Are they feeding you while you wait?"

"Water and peanuts. The big guy sitting next to me has eaten about 11,000 bags of peanuts."

"Sounds mighty appetizing. Logan wants to talk to you." He thinks it's cool to talk on the phone.

"Hi, Daddy. What are you doin'?"

"I'm in an airplane."

"Are you way up in the sky?"

"No, we're sitting on the ground."

"Daddy, airplanes are supposed to fly up in the sky."

"I'm well aware of that, Logan."

"Daddy, I'm the Blue Power Ranger."

"Yes, I know you are. Guess what? I'm on the same airplane with the Red Power Ranger. He's sitting right in front of me."

"No, you're not. The Red Power Ranger is on TV. Don't be stupid, Daddy."

Business travel sucks. For too many years, I flew to Atlanta, Chicago, Dallas, Huntsville, New York, Pittsburgh, San Antonio, and other cities for extended periods of time to work on information technology projects.

When I travel, I rarely order dinner from room service because I refuse to pay $42 for a cold cheeseburger and squishy fries. I usually go to a restaurant that's close to my hotel and try not to attract attention to myself. I'm always self-conscious because I feel as if everyone is staring at me and thinking, "Oh, that poor man doesn't have any family or friends, so he has to eat a giant slab of red meat, 64 home fries and an entire chocolate cake by himself. What a pathetic loser."

It never fails; the worst things happen when I'm away from home. A few years ago on a Sunday afternoon, I flew to Pittsburgh to prepare for a Monday morning meeting. I called home as soon as I got to my hotel to check in with my family. Starla answered the phone in tears.

"What's wrong?"

"There's a snake on the deck."

"What's it doing?"

"It's reading the newspaper, jerkwad. What do you think it's doing? It's slipping and sliding all over the place."

"Well, go out there and scare him away."

"I'm not going out there with that slimy thing. I hate it when you're gone." She burst into tears again. I felt horrible because I couldn't help her. The snake eventually slithered off the deck and everything was OK…until the next day. Monday afternoon I called home before I went out to dinner.

"Hi, it's me. How was your day?"

"Terrible. Tabitha bit Chase in preschool today. He has a set of teeth marks on his forearm."

"What happened?"

"Chase didn't want to play house with Tabitha, so she bit him. He got mad and tried to bite her back. The teacher caught him and gave him a time out." My young son had learned a valuable lesson about women: if you don't play house with them, they'll bite you.

Back on this God-forsaken airplane, the pilot just told us we would be stuck on the ground for at least another 45 minutes. That's just perfect. Now the workout enthusiast in the window seat smells like Shaquille O'Neal's sweat socks. The big fellow next to me has eaten every bag of peanuts on the plane and has now moved on to decimate the pretzel supply. Dylan is still the Red Power Ranger, and the engaged couple is squabbling about their wedding ceremony.

"Look, Todd, my father is shelling out $40,000 for our wedding. The least your family can do is fork over a paltry $10,000 for a nice rehearsal dinner."

"My family doesn't HAVE $10,000. Danielle, I need to tell you something: I've been thinking about this for a long time—I don't want to marry you."

Without saying a word, Danielle took a deep breath, gripped Todd's left hand tightly, and bit him in the forearm.

Boys and Girls Are Different—Duh

A few years ago, a group of child development researchers came to a startling conclusion: boys and girls are essentially similar. They said, "Given the same controlled living conditions, boys and girls will behave in a comparable manner."

When this research was released publicly, parents who actually live with children responded by saying, "That's the stupidest thing we've ever heard." The researchers were crushed by the idiocy of their conclusion and forced to leave their research jobs. Now they play musical spoons on the streets of Branson, Missouri.

Young girls are far more mature than boys. These charming young women are interested in building friendships, exploring their feelings, and learning new concepts every day. Young boys are interested in superheroes, Yu-Gi-Oh cards, and armpit farts. See, they're different—duh.

Starla often says, "Boys are disgusting...and they smell funny."

In defense of my gender, I always stand up to her and respond with strong conviction by saying, "Yes, Dear." Hey, I'm a man, but I'm not a fool.

Many boys lack sophistication. Oh, who the heck am I kidding? They're pigs and they grow up to be adult pigs. I'm a big ol' oinker and darned proud of it.

Case in point: Chase was invited to a birthday party for one of his classmates—a girl. Her name was...Britney...Tiffany...Amber...something like that. When we arrived at her home, we knew we were in trouble because her family had tied 20 pink balloons to her mailbox. This was going to get ugly. As we walked into the girl's home, Chase looked at me in panic and said, "Dad, this is a Barbie Princess Party. You gotta get me outta here, NOW!"

Although I agreed with him completely, I didn't want to hurt his friend's feelings, so I said, "Let's stay for the birthday cake. Then we'll leave." I can't pass up an opportunity for free cake.

One other boy, Tommy, came to the party, so at least my son had someone to share in his misery. Ten girls and two boys at a party—great odds if you're 19 years old but catastrophic when you're seven.

The girl's mother led us into her kitchen where she presented us with a lovely vegetable tray (including asparagus…really, no joke). My son looked at her as if she had four heads. "Do you have any chips or cookies?" he asked. Seemed like a valid question to me.

"Oh no, we are healthy eaters. The girls love broccoli and asparagus. We're vegans."

"Dad, they're aliens! We need to call the Men in Black," Chase whispered in horror.

"Vegan means they eat only natural foods like vegetables and fruit…and the Men in Black have an unlisted telephone number. Go find Tommy and try to have some fun."

The 10 girls sequestered themselves in the living room to play games centered on Barbie. I never knew she had so many careers: Flight Attendant, Rock Star, Model, Financial Advisor, Chemical Engineer, Nuclear Physicist, Astronaut, and many more. She looks so young, yet people say she is over 50. I bet she's had a lot of plastic surgery: a couple of facelifts, liposuction, botox, gastric bypass, and implants. There is a rumor going around that her old boyfriend Ken paid for the implants.

Have you ever noticed no one talks about Ken's profession? Did you know that he was a CPA in Arthur Andersen's Houston office? Although he wasn't directly involved in the Enron scandal, his career suffered for quite a while because of his Andersen affiliation. Currently, he is a senior manager with Ernst & Young (Tax and Audit) and shares a condo with Barbie's sister, Skipper. Evidently, Skipper provided Ken with a great deal of comfort (wink, wink, nudge, nudge) when Andersen collapsed. As usual, Barbie was away on business—a Space Shuttle Mission. Skipper and Barbie are not speaking to each other because Barbie doesn't approve of the relationship. I think she's just jealous. Ken doesn't like to talk about how his long-term relationship with Barbie ended. Some people say Barbie had a number of unresolved "issues" because Ken isn't anatomically correct.

I lost interest in the Barbie chat, so I made my way into the kitchen with the mommies. They were discussing their life experiences and the challenges they face as working mothers. It's intriguing to see how much women evolve and how little men seem to change over time. Let's take a hypothetical example: we'll begin with an excerpt from a conversation between two seven-year-old girls; we'll call them Ashley and Megan.

Ashley: "I like Barbie's blue dress. It's my favorite."

Megan: "I like Barbie's red dress. It looks nice on her." The girls continue to play quietly for a couple of hours and eventually break for a scrumptious snack of milk and cookies. What a lovely pair of young ladies.

Now for an excerpt from an imaginary conversation between two seven-year-old boys, let's say their names are Dylan and Evan.

Dylan: "The Flash can eat a hot dog faster than Superman."

Evan: "No way, butthead. Superman can eat a hot dog faster than the Flash."

Dylan: "I'm not a butthead. You're a butthead." A fight ensues. Fists fly from every direction. A lamp is broken, along with two teeth, a priceless vase and a 15-inch computer monitor. Immediately after the fight is over, the boys laugh and play video games.

Fast forward 30 years. This time we'll examine an excerpt from a conversation between the same two girls, Ashley and Megan, who are now 37 years old.

Ashley: "I don't know who I am. I try so hard to be a good mother, and I also want to have a successful career. It's a very difficult balancing act. I love my family, but my work is important to me. I'm torn between my two lives."

Megan: "Dr. Phil says your authentic self is the 'you' that can be found at your absolute core. It's the part of you that is not defined by your job, your function, or your role. It's the composite of all of your unique gifts, skills, abilities, interests, talents, insights, and wisdom. I think you should focus on finding your authentic self. Get in touch with the real you." See what I mean? These women have evolved into people who have highly developed cognitive skills and are willing to explore their emotional boundaries.

Finally, here is an excerpt from a hypothetical conversation between the two boys, Dylan and Evan, who are now 37 years old.

Dylan: "Michael Vick can run faster than Donovan McNabb."

Evan: "No way, you idiot, Donovan McNabb can run faster than Michael Vick."

Dylan: "I'm not an idiot. You're an idiot." A fight ensues. Fists fly from every direction, but none of them connect. A bag of Doritos is smashed. After 26 seconds, the men are exhausted. Immediately following the fight, they laugh and drink beer. I'm no expert, but I believe these guys have missed the evolution train.

This example proves the theory that men are from Mars, women are from Cleveland. No, that's not it. Men are from New Jersey; women are from a small town in Idaho. No, maybe it's…men are from Uranus…let's just stop right there.

Back at the Barbie Princess Party, I realized I had not seen Chase for 40 minutes so I went to look for him. He and Tommy avoided the Barbiefest and found a way to have a good time. They were in the backyard conducting a spitting contest. When the boys informed me they were competing for the World Spitting Championship, I felt the compelling need to enter the contest. I had to show them how the sport was meant to be played.

As my third and final loogie launch became airborne, the birthday girl's mother stepped through the back door and said, "Time for birthday cake!" Just as the words left her mouth, the liquid projectile plopped in the middle of an outdoor table about a foot away from her. She nearly gagged.

I took charge of the situation. "Boys, stop that this instant." I yelled. *Hey, I'm not taking the fall. They started it.* "Let's go in and have some cake." I turned to the mom and said, "Wonderful party." She didn't say anything but she had that "you are so disgusting" look on her face. I recognized it because I've seen that face on many women. As the boys ran inside, I whispered to them, "I'm the World Champion."

We gathered in the kitchen for birthday cake. I was hoping for a big chunk of chocolate. "I have a surprise for everyone," the mom said as she unveiled a giant cube made of an indeterminate off-white substance. The unnatural formation had seven birthday candles stuck in the middle. "It's a tofu birthday cake!" *You've got to be freakin' kidding me, lady.*

"Oh, my. I'm sorry we have to go now. I...um...just remembered I have to perform brain surgery in 15 minutes. Thanks for inviting us to the party. Happy birthday. Bye."

We bolted out of the house and jumped in our car. As we sped away, Chase said, "Dad, I didn't know you were a brain surgeon." *Oh boy, how am I going to explain this?*

"I'm an alien brain surgeon for the Men in Black. Don't tell anyone. It's a secret."

"OK, whatever," Chase said. *He probably thinks his dad is really weird.*

As you can clearly see, girls are significantly different from boys. Girls are complex, emotional creatures. Boys are simple animals, and they smell funny.

Oh yeah, and one more thing: Michael Vick **CAN** run faster than Donovan McNabb.

You're Just Going to
Feel a Little Pressure

On a warm Sunday afternoon last July, Starla went to the Baby Superstore to buy a present for a friend who was having a baby. Little did I know, this seemingly harmless shopping excursion set off a chain of events culminating in a incident that would inflict me with a humongous pain in the...no, not the neck...no, not in the butt...yes, in the you-know-whats.

After spending over two hours wandering through the Baby Superstore, Starla bounded through our front door with an armload of baby gifts. She dumped the presents on the kitchen table, collapsed on the couch, and said, "I love that store. It smells like newborn babies! Baby powder, baby lotion, baby clothes, baby booties. Don't you miss having a baby in the house?"

In my head, I heard an alarm sound. WARNING: Estrogen alert. Answer with extreme caution. "Um...well...we've already had two babies. Isn't that enough?"

She pled her case. "But babies are cuddly and soft and warm and lovable and..."

I interrupted, "...and expensive, and they cry a lot, and they grow into obnoxious three-year-olds, and they evolve into smelly seven-year-olds, and they transform into annoying teenagers, and they go to expensive private colleges, and..."

"But babies are so sweet. Don't you want to have just one more?"

"May I remind you that we are 41 years old? If we have another baby, we'll be 76 years old when he graduates from college."

"Sixty-three, Mr. Math Wiz."

"I bet we would feel like we're 76 by the time we put a third kid through college. Then he would probably come back to live at home! No thanks. I really think the baby factory needs to be put out of business."

"Well, if you feel that strongly about it, why don't you just go see your college buddy urologist, Dr. Willis, and get yourself a big ol' vasectomy?" she said as she turned and walked out of the room.

"All right, I will," I replied confidently. That felt good. I actually stood up for myself for once. Hey, wait a minute. What did I just commit to? Maybe I should have researched this procedure before I volunteered so eagerly.

Over the following week, Starla and I discussed this choice thoroughly and finally came to the conclusion that I would move forward with the idea. I scheduled an appointment with my friend, Dr. Stan Willis, and two weeks later I was sitting in his office for an initial consultation.

"So, are you absolutely sure you want to have a vasectomy?" Stan asked.

"Yes, Starla and I have talked about it, and we believe it's the right decision for us. I'm ready to do this."

"OK, take your pants off."

"Look, Stan, you're a good friend and all, but I'm not into that kind of thing."

"No, no, I need to examine you. It's for the procedure."

I dropped my trousers and stared out the window in humiliation as he examined me. Stan explained how the male physiology works as he proceeded with his assessment. Halfway through the process, Stan got the bright idea to initiate some idle chitchat.

"Last week I went to San Francisco for a medical conference. Beautiful city. On Thursday night, I went to a San Francisco Giants baseball game. They were playing the Dodgers. I got there early to watch Barry Bonds take batting practice. Man, that guy is powerful. He can really crush the ball."

I continued my stare out the window. "Stan, could you do me a favor? While you're doing whatever it is you're doing down there, could you please refrain from using the words CRUSH and BALL in the same sentence?"

Stan finished his assessment and described the procedure to me. "A vasectomy is the process of separating the vas, the tube that delivers the little soldiers to their intended destination, so you can prevent conception. It is the most common method of male contraception in this country. About 500,000 vasectomies are done each year. Because a vasectomy simply interrupts the delivery of your Olympic swimmers, it will not affect hormonal function, and your sexual ability will remain completely intact. Vasectomy is widely thought to be free of known long-term side effects, and is considered by most experts to be the safest and most reliable method of permanent male sterilization."

I felt much better about the procedure. "OK. So far so good. Keep going," I said.

"The traditional vasectomy is a minor surgical procedure that can be performed either in my office under local anesthetic or in an outpatient surgery center with full anesthesia. The choice is yours. Most of my patients have it done here in my office because it is more convenient for them. It takes about an hour to complete. I'll use a scalpel to make one or two incisions in the skin to access the tiny vas tubes on each side. Then I'll lift, cut, tie, and cauterize the vas tubes. I'll return the tubes to their original position and close the incisions with three or four stitches."

My eyes must have been the size of commemorative Elvis plates. "Stan, this sounds...[gulp]...very painful," I whispered.

"You're just going to feel a little pressure at first. Then the local anesthetic will kick in and you'll be fine. Do you want to do it here in my office?"

"Um...yeah...I guess so." Stan's spicy blonde administrative assistant, Bernadette, scheduled a date and time for my procedure, and I walked out of his office like a zombie. As I drove home, my brain worked relentlessly to process some critical words from Stan's explanation. Scalpel. Incisions. Cut. Tie. Cauterize. Stitches. I replayed Stan's words of comfort over and over. "You're just going to feel a little pressure. You'll be fine." I kept telling myself I would be OK. I can do this.

Three weeks later on a rainy Friday morning, I found myself sitting on Stan's exam table wearing only a flimsy gown and a pair of white sox. After 38 unbearable minutes, Stan entered the room and geared up for the procedure. He told me to lie down and relax. Yeah, right, I hadn't been able to relax for the past three weeks, and I sure as heck wasn't going to start now. Stan "prepped" me by shaving the area, which was a very strange experience. Stan and I had been friends for more than 20 years, and this activity pegged into the red zone of the weird-o-meter.

Stan picked up a hypodermic needle that was about a yard long and reassured me by saying, "OK, you're just going to feel a little pressure now." He inserted the needle into my [you know where] and AAAARRRRRGGGGHHHH! I thought I was going to DIE! The pain went waaaaaaay beyond excruciating. It felt like he had clubbed me in the crotch with a 10-pound sledge hammer. Stan told me I would just feel a little pressure. Taking the CPA exam makes you feel a little pressure. Stubbing your pinky toe on a coffee table makes you feel a little pressure. Speaking in front of 10,000 people while you are wearing only a pair of leopard skin bikini underwear makes you feel a little pressure. That freakin' needle hurt like hell.

The pain got worse. I thought Stan had pulled my little tubes completely out of my body and used them as jump ropes. He tugged and snipped and tied and cauterized until I nearly fell into a pain coma.

Stan finished the last stitch and admired his handiwork. "That's it. I'm all done. Now that wasn't so bad, was it?" he said.

"Stan, that was the worst experience I've ever had in my life."

"Your pain threshold is pretty low. We probably should have done this in a surgery center with full anesthesia." *What is the penalty for second degree murder in the Commonwealth of Virginia?*

"You'll be sore for a few days. Don't run or do any heavy lifting."

"I can barely sit up and you're telling me not to run? Gee, thanks for the advice, Doc."

"Use the pain medicine I have prescribed for you and keep an ice pack on the area for the next couple of days. You should be able to go back to work on Monday. Come back and see me for a follow-up exam in two weeks."

I was in agony the entire weekend. My noogies were swollen like two over-filled water balloons. The pain medicine helped a little, but not nearly enough.

At work on Monday morning, I walked through the office like I had two basketballs in my pants. My executive assistant, Kim, noticed I was walking funny and asked, "What happened to you?"

"Oh, I was…playing racquetball at the gym on Saturday and pulled a groin." Big mistake. When the guys on *SportsCenter* say, "Emmitt Smith pulled a groin," it sounds like a normal sports injury. When I said it, I sounded like a middle-aged man making up an excuse to cover up the fact that his plumbing had been permanently rearranged.

For the next two weeks, I moseyed around the office like a bowlegged cowboy. My coworkers called me Tex and asked me where I had parked my horse. Kim offered me a shot of whiskey. Every time I saw Mark Huffman in the hall, he yelled, "Draw, partner" or "Reach for the sky, ya pesky varmint." I hate him.

I returned to Stan's office, as scheduled, for my follow-up visit. He told me I was healing properly and my procedure was a resounding success. During my exam, I noticed Stan seemed distant, as if he was preoccupied with a personal problem.

"Stan, is something bothering you?" I asked.

"Yeah. A couple of days ago, my wife caught me in bed with Bernadette. This makes the third time she has caught me cheating on her. She says she's going to file for divorce and take everything I own. How could I have been so stupid?"

I offered my judgment-impaired friend some words of encouragement. "Don't worry, Stan. I'm sure everything will work out fine. You're just going to feel a little pressure."

Take My Advice, Please

Why do so many people feel the need to blurt out unsolicited advice? It rarely turns out to be good, and most of the time their recommendations lead to disaster. Suggestions such as "Leonard, I bet you'd look mighty handsome with one of those fancy mullet haircuts," or "Luther, you should be honest with your wife and let her know that her thighs look like tree trunks," will only inflict pain and suffering on every party involved.

Bad advice has been around since the beginning of human existence. The first person to utter a piece of bad advice was Eve in the Garden of Eden. After feasting on the forbidden apple, Eve proceeded to give Adam some advice that changed the course of mankind.

Eve: "Adam, you have to taste this apple. It's delicious. You'll love it."

Adam: "Didn't God tell us NOT to eat the apple?"

Eve: "Don't be a weenie. Eat it."

Adam: "What's a weenie?"

Eve: "Never mind. Just eat the stupid apple. It's fat free."

As Adam chomped into the illegal fruit, an ominous feeling of transgression encompassed his body, and he realized they weren't wearing any fig leaves.

Adam: "Eve, we're naked! Wanna fool around?"

Eve: "Don't touch me. I'm bloated."

The specter of bad advice continued through the ages as humans throughout the world listened to incompetent advisors. Think about the Native Americans who sold Manhattan Island to a group of white settlers in the early 1600s. What kind of loony advice did Chief Soaring Eagle get from his senior financial consultant, Constipated Otter?

Chief Soaring Eagle: "The settlers want to buy our island. How much should we charge them?"

Constipated Otter: "$16."

Chief Soaring Eagle: "That doesn't sound like much money. Plus, we'll have to pay our real estate agent his 6% commission, which will eat into our profit."

Constipated Otter: "Don't worry. I came up with a plan to invest the money we have left over. My brother-in-law, Squatting Bear, is a stock broker, and he gave me a tip on a company that can't lose. We'll be rich. Trust me."

Chief Soaring Eagle: "What company is it?"

Constipated Otter: "WorldCom."

The subject of parenting generates mountains of lousy advice. I've encountered hundreds of people (all right, not hundreds, maybe six) who believed they were child development experts and felt compelled to tell me how to raise my children. From the controversial spanking vs. timeout debate to the environmental dispute over cloth and disposable diapers, all people seem to have an opinion, and for some bizarre reason, they think I want to hear it.

One morning I was in a conference room, waiting for a useless meeting to start. A young analyst, Lynn, came into the room and asked me how my morning was going.

"Oh, just peachy. I had two knock-down-drag-out fights with my three-year-old, Logan, this morning. He nearly made me late for work."

"Over what?" she asked.

"Well, to start the day off, he didn't want to wear his pants. I had to chase him all over the house, wrestle him into submission, and force his pants on as he kicked me repeatedly in the stomach. Then, as if that wasn't enough torment, he refused to sit in his car seat. I spent 15 minutes trying to reason with the irrational ogre, until finally I had to bribe him with a Blueberry Pop Tart to get him to sit down."

Lynn shook her head in disapproval. "Your approach is all wrong. You need to give him options. That way he can feel empowered to make decisions that directly affect his life."

"Options, huh? OK, what options could I have given him? I couldn't take him to preschool with no pants. His teachers require the use of pants. Most importantly, Starla would kick my butt if she found out I took him to school without his pants. Now, let's talk about the car seat. Kids have to ride in a car seat to be safe. There are no options. I'm not going to endanger my child just because he doesn't want to buckle up. Do you have any kids?"

"No, but I took a child development class my sophomore year in college, and I read an article on parenting in *Cosmo* last week. I treat my dog like a child."

"Oh yeah, you're a regular Mr. Spock."

"That's Dr. Spock."

"Whatever. I think I'll just continue to get my parenting instruction from a qualified child development professional: Andy Griffith."

In an effort to provide you with good parenting guidance you can use in your everyday life, I have assembled my top 10 pieces of advice for dads:

1. Never turn your back on a three-year-old when he is holding a garden hose.

2. Don't send your son to a summer camp called "Flower Arranging Can Be Fun."

3. Feel free to consider ketchup to be a vegetable.

4. Stop saying, "Is anyone listening to me?" Here's a news flash. No one is listening to you.

5. Caution: Barbie doll heads detonate when you throw them into a bonfire.

6. Go with your instincts. You're absolutely right; the Teletubbies are creepy.

7. No one can explain why Scrappy Doo speaks perfectly, while his uncle, Scooby Doo, has a horrible speech impediment. Stop trying to figure it out. Just accept it and get on with your life.

8. Video games will make your kids more intelligent. Keep repeating this statement over and over until you believe it. It won't be true, but you'll feel better when your kid plays *Laura Croft Tomb Raider* for nine hours straight without stopping to eat or go to the bathroom.

9. The Tooth Fairy will give your kids more money for a lost tooth than you got when you were a kid. It's called inflation. Stop complaining about it.

10. Never take financial advice from a guy named Constipated Otter.

Television...Is Nothing Sacred?

For years, hordes of child development researchers have told us how detrimental television can be to our children. Some people say watching too much television will turn a kid's brain to mush. I don't agree. When I was a kid, I watched a ton of television and look how I turned out...um...maybe I'm a bad example.

I grew up in a small agricultural community in Southwestern Virginia called Floyd County. The rural countryside rolls for miles, and a solitary stoplight directs traffic at the only major intersection in the county. Southern hospitality is a part of the genetic code of the locals, along with NASCAR, pickup trucks, and banana pudding with lots of vanilla wafers.

I was a child in the '60s, but I wasn't a hip, with-it kind of kid. My sister, Bonnie, was the cool one in the family—not me. I had buckteeth, Coke bottle glasses, and an unhealthy fixation on television. While the rest of the world dealt with civil unrest, I watched *Ed Sullivan* and *Laugh-In*. At that time, the only national television networks in operation were NBC, CBS, PBS, and ABC. My family lived so far out in the country that our puny TV antenna received just the local NBC and CBS affiliates based in Roanoke. The PBS signal was way too snowy to watch, and the transmission from the ABC affiliate in Lynchburg didn't have the strength to reach us. I spent my childhood as a geeky kid living in the mountains, stuck with two channels. When the President appeared on television to give a speech to the American public, I was screwed.

Now my kids have a zillion TV channels to surf through. They don't understand the pain and suffering I went through as a kid. We didn't have a remote control. I had to get up and walk to the TV...uphill both ways...in the snow...with no shoes on...to change the channel. I can still feel the chill in my knees.

As I got older, my thirst for television grew into an obsession. *Love Boat, Sanford and Son, The Dukes of Hazzard*—I watched them all and laughed myself silly. After minutes of protracted research, I have found I am not alone in my fascination with television. Millions of men all over the world share my passion for the boob tube. Why do you think *Baywatch* was a giant international success? Duh. We are visual creatures. Guys like to look at stuff.

Dr. Phil says, "Women fall in love with their ears." They respond to verbal stimulation and lively conversation. Men fall in love with their...eyes (you thought I was going to say something else, didn't you?). This verbal vs. visual divergence explains why men have problems meeting women. I'll demonstrate. Let's say a man is in a grocery store and sees an attractive woman in the fresh fruit section with an impressive set of cantaloupes. His visual stimulation meter goes off the scale. He walks over to her and tries to start a conversation.

"Hi. I couldn't help noticing you have beautiful melons. May I thump them?"

The woman's verbal stimulation meter identifies him as a PERVERT. She tells the store security guard about a strange man lurking in the produce section. The guard escorts the man out of the store and calls the police. In this example, the man should have stayed home and watched *The Dukes of Hazzard* with Catherine Bach in her Daisy Duke shorts. This way, his need for visual stimulation would have been satisfied, and he would not be classified as an incompetent sexual predator.

The male fascination with television starts at a very early age. Toddlers get hooked on *Sesame Street, Teletubbies,* and the *Wiggles.* As they get older, they move on to *Power Rangers* and *Scooby Doo.* Eventually, they graduate to *Justice League* and *Spiderman.* Starla and I try to read books to the kids every day and encourage them to find various ways to entertain themselves, but eventually their attention always returns to television. This fascination has become a problem. With the advent of cable and satellite television, cartoons are now available 24 hours a day. My kids are fully aware of the Cartoon Network schedule, and they're eating into my TV time. It's a travesty.

Don't get me wrong, I love to watch the new *Justice League* cartoon or the classic *Space Ghost,* but my kids insist on watching these new-fangled cartoons from Japan like *Pokémon, Digimon, Yu-Gi-Oh, Dragonball Z, G Gundam, Yuyu Hakusho,* and *Rurouni Kenshin.* I can't tell them apart, and all the characters do is fight. No plot, no character development, just lots of fighting. Sort of like an animated version of professional wrestling in Japanese. My kids have even picked up Japanese phrases and constantly say them around the house. I don't know if they're complimenting me or mocking me. I shouldn't be so stupid. Of course, they're mocking me. It's a bit disturbing to realize my kids are learning to speak Japanese, and I'm still struggling with English.

When my kids get tired of Cartoon Network, they watch movies on DVD or videotape...ON MY TV. This preoccupation is especially annoying when you have a three-year-old, because kids this age can watch the same movie four times a day, every day, for six weeks. I have seen *Lion King* more than 7,000 times. I don't mind watching the good movies like *Aladdin, Men in Black*, and *Shrek,* but watching a two-hour *Pokémon* movie twice a day for three weeks turned me into a blubbering fool. I still have nightmares about that little yellow *Pokémon* called Pikachu. He's evil. I think he's trying to control my mind. He keeps telling me to buy him a car. Maybe I need therapy.

On the rare occasions when I seize control of the TV, the boys find ways to make my viewing experience as agonizing as possible. They play with the loudest toys they own, yell at the top of their lungs, conduct boxing matches, and stand directly in front of me saying, "Dad, look what I can do." For the past six years, I haven't heard a complete sentence of TV dialogue while my kids have been in the living room.

Before Chase was born, I was an *X-Files* fanatic. I watched every show and attempted to keep up with the complicated plot twists that made the show famous. I stayed current on the storyline until about six years ago when Chase started talking. He hasn't stopped since. I tried to watch the *X-Files*, but that little rascal, Chase, found every way humanly possible to distract me at critical points in the show. Technically, I "saw" the shows, but I couldn't hear a thing Mulder and Scully said. I have no idea what happened to Mulder. Where the heck did he go? Lately, I have been trying to find information on the Internet to help me fill in the blanks on the *X-Files* series. Man, I am such a geek.

To combat the noise, I had to change my television viewing preferences to include shows that do not require the existence of dialogue. My favorite shows are *Baywatch, Xena, Baywatch, Charlie's Angels, Baywatch, Star Trek,* and *Baywatch.*

Sometimes Starla makes the mistake of trying to talk to me over the commotion created by the boys and the television. Just the other day, I was watching *Baywatch* and the boys were fighting over a Spiderman action figure. Starla stepped into the living room and said, "Honey, can we talk about our relationship? I'd like to get an understanding of your feelings at this point in the progression of our life as a couple."

"What? I can't hear a word you're saying," I yelled over the racket.

"Oh, never mind. What do you want for dinner?' she asked.

"For some reason, I have a strong craving for cantaloupes."

My Wife Is Cool Toy Challenged

Halloween is a wonderful tradition. It gives children the opportunity to dress up in fun costumes, destroy their neighbors' landscaping, and collect tons of chocolate that is eaten by their fathers after they go to bed.

Unfortunately, Halloween also has a dark side. No, I don't mean the celebration of hideous mythical creatures like Dracula, Frankenstein, and Michael Jackson. I'm talking about mothers who dress their young sons in stupid costumes. Every Halloween throughout the country, mothers create embarrassing costumes for toddlers who don't have the ability to fight back. I believe it creates a feeling of low self-esteem for the toddlers and bugs the heck out of dads. It's an epidemic that must be stopped.

Last year for Halloween, we took our kids to a neighbor's house for a party. My two boys were dressed as Batman and Batman—not a lot of originality, but good masculine costumes. Our neighbor, Deborah, greeted us at the door, holding her two-year-old son, Trevor. The toddler was wearing an orange velour jumpsuit and a green beret.

"Oh, doesn't he look darling?" Starla said as she gave the woman one of those envious "You are soooooo pre-indictment Martha Stewart" looks.

"What is he supposed to be, a French Interior Designer?" I asked.

"No, you silly goose. He's a carrot!" Deborah squealed.

I stared at Trevor's dad, Lawrence, in disbelief. "Yeah, he's a freakin' carrot. Don't even start with me," Lawrence said as he took another shot of Tequila.

The humiliated toddler's mother took about seven billion pictures of him, which I'm sure will end up in the hands of his worst enemies in high school. No good will come of this horror. Won't you please help stop this travesty by sending me $4,000? No checks—cash only. I promise I'll contemplate this problem as I sit on a Caribbean beach and pound shots of Tequila with Lawrence in an effort to help him defeat this awful condition. Please, help us today so we can book our flight early and reserve good hotel rooms overlooking the water.

This type of crisis is not confined to the Halloween season. After a great deal of research (actually, I thought about this while I was watching the *Today* show), I have noticed that many mothers have difficulty identifying boy-appropriate merchandise—specifically action figures. These women are Cool Toy Challenged.

There is a plethora (fancy word—I have a thesaurus) of toys available for kids. Selecting cool boy-appropriate toys can be a tricky task, especially for moms who aren't familiar with popular cartoon characters. Although the Power Puff Girls are superheroes, most boys do not have an interest in playing with action figures named Blossom, Buttercup, and Bubbles. Wonder Woman, also a superhero, tends to capture the attention of older boys (read: dads) because of her amazing…um…physical assets.

Starla is severely Cool Toy Challenged. For Chase's fourth birthday, she made a futile attempt to select a cool toy for him. She came home from the toy store bursting with excitement. "I found the most wonderful gift for Chase," she said. She reached into her shopping bag and pulled out a Batman action figure. It had the usual Batman cowl, cape, and lots of muscles, but his suit was…[Gasp]…lavender.

"Honey, I hate to break this to you, but Batman does not wear a LAVENDER BATSUIT!"

"It's a beautiful shade and Batman has dark features, so the lavender will accentuate the natural coloring in his face. The other Batman toys were black. Although black is slimming, I think lavender makes him look fun and frisky."

"Batman is NOT frisky. He's the Dark Knight. The Caped Crusader. Very serious."

"Well then, he needs to lighten up and put on a happy face. Lavender will give him a playful flair."

A playful flair? This is blasphemy to those of us who have followed his adventures over the years. Why, it would almost give the impression that Batman was a little…light in the Batboots. Not that there's anything wrong with that. What if the Dark Knight embraced an alternative lifestyle? Let's look at one possible scenario.

It's 10:30 PM at Stately Wayne Manor just outside of Gotham City. Billionaire Bruce Wayne and his young ward, Dick Grayson, are watching *Beaches* on DVD. The violet Batphone rings. It's Commissioner Gordon with shocking news—the Joker has kidnapped the five stars of the television show *Queer Eye for the Straight Guy*. Just in case you haven't heard about this new reality show, five gay men redecorate a straight man's home and give him a complete makeover. The show is simply fabulous.

"We're on our way, Commissioner," Bruce says as he activates the secret entrance to the Batcave behind a life-size painting of Liza Minnelli. Bruce and

Dick slide down the Batpoles [insert your own joke here] into the Batdressing room. Tonight, Bruce chooses a sequined cowl with a matching cape and a Donna Karan utility belt. Dick picks a feathered mask he wears when he works as a backup dancer for Cher.

Ready for battle, they burst out of the Batcloset into the Batcave, which is festooned elegantly in an explosion of spring pastels. The crime fighters leap into the Batmobile. Batman turns to Robin and says, "Do I detect the scent of potpourri?"

"I used Febreeze on the upholstery this morning," Robin says proudly.

"Nice going, old chum." They speed through the night as Barbra Streisand's "Happy Days Are Here Again" blares out of the Batmobilestereo. They arrive at the Joker's lair on Hudson Avenue, and sneak in through an open door.

"Holy window treatments, Batman! This place looks like it was decorated by Richard Simmons on crack," exclaims Robin, the Flamboyant Wonder. His eyes grow with amazement at the lack of thought that went into the décor of the Joker's secret hideaway. The mauve carpet didn't go with the light blue walls. The couch was some awful off-green that doesn't exist in nature and the lamps looked like K-Mart rejects.

They hear screams coming from a rear bedroom. Batman kicks down the door with a spiffy move he learned in his Tae-Bo class. As the superheroes run into the bedroom, they are shocked to see the five television stars tied to cold metal chairs with floral scarves. They are facing a television and their faces are saturated with disgust.

"What's going on here, Batman?" asks Robin.

"They're being forced to watch an unimaginably hideous sight against their will. Oh, the carnage is unbearable." Batman winces in pain.

For six hours, the Joker had forced the five television stars to watch reruns of the classic television show *Petticoat Junction*. Kyan Douglas, the grooming guru, was absolutely appalled at Uncle Joe's hair care habits—no wonder he was movin' kinda slow. Ted Allen, a food and wine connoisseur, couldn't believe human beings would actually eat biscuits lathered with sausage gravy. Design Doctor, Thom Filicia, contracted a rash from the metal chair. Carson Kressley, the show's fashion savant, went into convulsions when he saw the plain dresses worn by the Bradley girls (Betty Jo, Bobbie Jo, and Billie Jo). Culture Vulture, Jai Rodriguez, watched in astonishment as the girls took baths in a tower containing the town's water supply. None of the five men could understand why anyone would want to live in a city named Hooterville.

The Joker surprises the Courageous Crime-fighting Couple from behind and says, "I see you've found my houseguests, Batman."

"Joker, why are you doing this?" Batman asks the cagey criminal.

"For 20 years, I've worked my buns off to overcome the sweeping gay generalizations that run rampant in the straight community. Now these five men are appearing on television and perpetuating the very stereotypes I've been trying to kill. I'm not going to let them do it. I'm going to torment them forever."

"You'll never get away with this, Joker. And by the way...you're wearing way too much makeup."

"I'm a Super Villain. I'm proud. Get used to it. Get 'em boys." The Joker's henchmen, dressed in pea-green jumpsuits and matching Candies Filly Suede boots attack the Dynamic Duo.

"POW! SOCKO! I'll give you such a pinch. KABLAMO! You're messing up my hair. ZING! That's gonna leave a mark. SPLATT!" The Caped Crusaders easily dispense with the henchmen and set the five television stars free.

"It's over, Joker. We're taking you to the State Penitentiary," Batman says, wiping his brow with a Vera Wang Batglove.

"All right, you got me this time, Batman. But can we stop at Starbucks on the way? I'm dying for a latte." They drive into the darkness singing "It's Raining Men." Once again, Gotham City is safe.

As you can see, a Cool Toy Challenged mother can dramatically change the action figure world as we know it. To help my wife restrain this awful affliction, I have assumed the duty of purchasing all action figures for my sons. In fact, just the other day, I picked up an exquisite lilac Spiderman.

There's No Place Like Home for the Holidays

Ah, the holiday season. What a joyous time of the year. A time to give thanks for the best things in life: your loving family, close friends, and the Wonder Bra.

Thanksgiving signals the beginning of the holiday season and always creates a major dilemma in our family. Where will we have Thanksgiving dinner? Which family member will be bold enough (or stupid enough) to volunteer to host the event? The host must assume responsibility for the meal and endure the punishment of having wacky family members, kids, and dogs ransack the home they have worked so hard to build. Last year, Starla felt the pressure to volunteer for the task.

Thanksgiving morning arrived with a slight chill in the air. By 9:00 AM, 10 adults, four boys, and two St. Bernard puppies filled our house. Everyone performed his or her assigned duty. Starla and her three sisters cooked frantically in the kitchen. My mother-in-law, Nana, pleaded for someone to provide her with a granddaughter. Papa George watched the Weather Channel and fell asleep on the couch. My three brothers-in-law and I sequestered ourselves in the garage and peered into the engine of my car, pretending we had a clue how the darned thing worked. The boys transformed our formal living room furniture into an obstacle course, and the dogs used my recliner as a teething toy. The "puppies" (Slimer and Poots) were only 11 months old, but they each weighed over 120 pounds. Within 15 minutes, my favorite chair was covered with drool and smelled like a wet dog. Oh, how I love the holiday season.

After five hours of drudgery in the kitchen, Starla and her sisters completed their monumental undertaking. Time to strap on the feedbag. I surveyed the dining room table heaped with Southern delicacies like homemade biscuits and cornbread. Then I casually mentioned, "Starla, I'm on this low carbohydrate Atkins diet, so I can't eat any bread, potatoes, or rice. Could you please make me some bacon and eggs?"

Starla, exhausted from her work in the kitchen, just shook her head and muttered, "Shut up and eat." I'm no psychic, but I think she was mad at me.

My sons took the situation from bad to worse. Chase stared at the feast of turkey, mashed potatoes, and corn on the cob. "Mom, can I have some peanut butter crackers and chips?" he asked.

Logan chimed in, "I want a peanut butter and jelly sandwich."

I could tell Starla's head was about to explode, so I decided to change the subject. I looked at my sister-in-law and said, "Soooooooo, Caroline, isn't it about time for you and Charlie to have a baby?" This statement set my mother-in-law into motion and she talked for 25 minutes about how much she needed a granddaughter.

I topped off my meal with a colossal wedge of Aunt Becky's chocolate pie (screw the diet—it's a family tradition) and rapidly fell asleep in my canine-scented recliner. I needed my rest because the following day we were scheduled to go Christmas shopping.

The Friday after Thanksgiving is the biggest shopping day of the year. Every year, throngs of humanity plow, shove, and cuss their way through gigantic malls in an attempt to find perfect gifts—or at least something on sale.

Before Starla and I set out on our shopping expedition, I asked Logan what he wanted for Christmas. At the time, he was enamored with the *Toy Story* movies. I'll admit I love them too. The main characters in these movies are Buzz Lightyear (a space ranger) and Sheriff Woody (a cowboy). The three-year-old pondered my question for a nanosecond and stated, "All I want for Christmas is a big Buzz and a big Woody."

Our hunting trip began at Toys "R" Us. We pushed our way through the store looking for the *Toy Story* action figures. Along the way, I picked up some presents for Chase, including a *Star Wars* Lego set, a computer game, and a cool Batmobile. The great thing about having boys is you can buy all of the stuff you wanted as a kid.

We jostled our way to the *Toy Story* section. The shelves were filled with characters from the movies: Mr. Potato Head, RC the remote controlled car, Rex the Dinosaur, and Slinky the Dog. Of course, the Buzz Lightyear and Sheriff Woody toys were sold out. I found a store employee and asked, "When do you think you'll have more *Toy Story* merchandise?"

"When the truck brings them from the warehouse," he replied. *Well, duh, doofus.*

"And when will that be?" I said as I tried to restrain my frustration.

"I dunno. Some days the truck comes and some days it don't." *I hate shopping.*

We took our items to the front of the store and stood in a checkout line behind approximately two billion people, all of whom paid by check. We waited so long, I grew a beard. By the time we got through the line, our clothes were out of style.

We went to five more toy stores looking for Buzz Lightyear and Sheriff Woody. Our last resort was Target. We scanned the toy section and found a huge selection of Buzz and Woody toys. Starla and I high-fived each other as we boogied to the checkout counter. We love Target—it's the best store in the whole wide world. (Attention: Target executives: How's that for a testimonial? Please send cash.)

The next four weeks passed quickly, and Santa Claus delivered a great haul of presents for the boys. At 6:00 AM on Christmas morning, they ran downstairs to find their presents under the tree. I gave Logan a big Daddy hug, "Merry Christmas! What do you think Santa brought you?"

"All I want for Christmas is a Transformer."

"Huh? I thought you wanted Buzz and Woody."

"No. I want a Transformer." *Oh boy.*

He opened his presents and found a *Spiderman* puzzle, an *X-Men* game, and a Tonka Truck. Finally, he opened his biggest present which was covered in *Toy Story* wrapping paper.

"ALL RIGHT!! Buzz and Woody," he yelled. Thank goodness he forgot all about the Transformer. He gave the box to me and said, "Open it, Daddy." I ripped it open to find Buzz Lightyear strapped to the back of the box with 400 steel bands, 138 iron plates, and a titanium alloy locking mechanism. I worked for an hour trying to free Buzz from his container. After I broke through the last steel band, I gently handed Buzz to my son. "Thanks, Daddy." Crack. He broke Buzz's head off. "Daddy, can you fix him?"

For the next hour I worked to reattach Buzz's head with superglue and duct tape. "Here you go. Be careful." I gave him the toy and Buzz's head fell off again.

"Where's my Transformer?" Logan asked.

Just then the doorbell rang. Our neighbors, Kristen and Wilber, burst through the front door with armloads of presents for the boys. Because they don't have kids, Kristen and Wilber always shower our boys with gifts. They mean well, but they are inexperienced at buying parent-friendly toys.

Wilber gave Chase a huge package to open. It was a fire truck with a real siren…a LOUD siren. A siren that Chase blew over and over and over until my ears started to bleed.

Then Wilber handed Logan a gift wrapped in bright yellow paper. Logan tore it apart to find a Bob the Builder tool set that included a hammer. A hammer. That dumbass Wilber gave my three-year-old a freakin' HAMMER! It had a horn in it, so when Logan hit something, it would make a loud HONK noise. Of course, Logan ran around the house smacking everything he could reach. HONK. HONK. HONK. HONK. The situation deteriorated into a Master-Card commercial:

- Expensive lamp in the formal living room: $260.

- 17-inch flat panel computer monitor: $140.

- Seeing Logan crack Wilber in the groin with that stupid hammer: priceless.

After dinner, Kristen and Wilber went home and we put the boys to bed. It was time for Starla and me to exchange Christmas presents. I gave her the tennis bracelet she told me to buy for her. She gave me socks and underwear.

"I never know what to get you for Christmas," she said.

I winked at her. "All I want for Christmas is a big buzz and a big woody."

Huh... What?

The average human brain is approximately the size of a grapefruit and weighs about three pounds. The brain is made up of tiny cells called neurons. More than 100 billion brain neurons send and receive electro-chemical signals through the central nervous system at speeds of over 200 MPH. Unfortunately, the neurons in my brain are heavily influenced by two rebel brain cells called morons named Leroy and Edgar who constantly try to persuade my neurons to fly to Vegas for the weekend and spend all of my money on booze, blackjack, and the buffet at the Bellagio.

Although a woman's brain and a man's brain are somewhat similar in nature, they have significant differences in their designs. The largest part of the human brain is called the cerebrum. A woman's cerebrum consists of four lobes, including the Get Out of Here I'm Taking a Shower Lobe, the Don't Even Think About Walking Through My Clean House With Mud on Your Shoes Lobe, the Put Your Plate in the Dishwasher Lobe, and, of course, the Brad Pitt Lobe. A man's cerebrum has two lobes; the Oh Yeah, Baby, I'm Thinking About Sex Lobe occupies 88% of the male brain, and the Everything Else Lobe inhabits 2% of the area. The remaining 10% of the male brain is reserved for later use and labeled "Future Site of Dreams About Supermodel Heidi Klum."

The cerebrum is divided into two hemispheres, often referred to as the right brain and the left brain. The right brain controls our creative processes and allows us to be artistic, musical, spatial, and intuitive. The left brain is rational and helps us to be linear, objective, analytical, and linguistic. In a woman's brain, the hemispheres are connected by tissue that conducts neural pathways and transmits data at the speed of light between the hemispheres. This broadband connection between hemispheres gives women the ability to process multiple thoughts and perform a multitude of different activities at the same time. Their multitasking capabilities are legendary and seem to become more pronounced after they have children. In a man's brain, the hemispheres are coupled with dried-up caulk and duct tape. We can focus on only one task at a time, and if we are interrupted while we are working on the task, our brain experiences a fatal error. The male brain must then reboot and start over from the beginning of the task.

Because our brains are wired differently, communication between a man and a woman can become strained, if not impossible, at times. One day last January, I was watching an interesting little TV show called *The Super Bowl*. In the middle of the third quarter, Starla walked over to my recliner and said, "Can you call the plumber tomorrow morning and ask him if he can fix our bathroom tile, and can you replace the burned out light bulb in the hall? Do you want meatloaf or chicken for dinner? Meatloaf takes longer because I have to mix it up, and I hate to get my hands messy in the meat. Chicken is easier and it has less fat. Logan needs new shoes for school. I'm having lunch with Sandy next Saturday. She just went on a trip to Atlantic City. Where do you want to go on vacation this year? So can you call the plumber tomorrow morning?"

"Huh…what?"

"You didn't hear a single word I said, did you?"

"Tampa Bay just got another interception," I said with excitement. For some reason, she didn't seem to care about the Tampa Bay Buccaneers. She was smart enough to quit while she was behind and left me alone with the game.

Starla's ability to process multiple simultaneous thoughts is available 24/7. She can also function at a high level in the wee hours of the morning. She is a pre-op nurse and opens her surgery center at 6:30 AM, which means she has to leave for work at the ungodly hour of 5:45 AM. One morning last winter, she woke me up from a deep sleep at 5:40 AM with the following directions:

"Wake up! Chase had a fever last night. If he still has a fever when he wakes up, give him two teaspoons of Children's Tylenol. Check his throat to make sure it doesn't have white spots in the back. Ask him if his stomach hurts, and check to see if his glands are swollen. If he's really sick, call the pediatrician's office and get an appointment for this morning. Ask for Dr. Engoiagln or Dr. Bagtolokit-karswarian. Do not let them book you with Dr. Venkateshsuari because I work with him every Thursday and he's a jerkwad."

My bleary eyes could barely distinguish her features, and I was in a state of shock because she rudely interrupted a really good Heidi Klum dream. "Huh…what?" I said in a sleepy stupor. As she ran out the door, I turned over and quickly went back to sleep. Sadly, Heidi was gone.

When Chase woke up, he said, "Dad, I don't feel so good."

I knew I was supposed to do something, but I couldn't for the life of me remember what it was. "Have some orange juice and a Flintstone's vitamin," I suggested. He chugged a big glass of juice and crunched the vitamin. After about 20 minutes, he felt better (whew). I called Starla to let her know that Chase was OK, and I did everything she told me to do (oh yeah, like you never told your spouse a little white lie to keep yourself out of trouble). Luck was with me that day.

Even though they are young, my sons also suffer from the male brain syndrome. One Saturday morning, they focused their attention on a new episode of *SpongeBob SquarePants*. At 10:38 AM, Starla made a sweeping announcement: "Boys, today is our clean-up day. Put your toys in the toy box and your socks in the clothes hamper. Shovel out your rooms, make your beds, and take a bath. Use soap this time. Hang up your towels, and please pee in the toilet—not just in the general vicinity."

To which, the boys replied, "Huh...what?" They were firmly locked into their *SpongeBob* trance, and it was going to take a mom explosion to get their attention. I knew this was going to get ugly, so I went outside to mow the grass and get out of the line of fire. An hour and a half later, I returned to see Starla had vacuumed the entire house, cleaned the bathrooms, washed three loads of clothes, folded the laundry, made lunch, picked up 638 toys, and replaced the burned-out light bulb in the hall. The freshly bathed boys actually smelled good for a change. How did she get all of that work done in such a short amount of time? One word: multitasking.

The other night, I tried to turn the tables on Starla and catch her in a moment of weakness to prove her abilities are not superhuman. She was relaxing on the couch watching *Trading Spaces*, a show on the Learning Channel in which two sets of neighbors work with professional interior decorators to completely transform a room in each other's home into a dreadful mess. Hosted by perky Paige Davis, the show illustrates ridiculous home decorating ideas no real person would ever inflict on an unsuspecting house. From painting a room baby diarrhea brown to stapling 6,000 fake flowers on the bathroom walls, these people come up with the silliest home decorating concepts imaginable. At the beginning of this particular episode, a woman stated emphatically, "Don't paint my walls green. I hate green. Please, I'm begging you, paint them any color but green." The decorator had a flash of inspiration and exclaimed, "I have a great idea. We're gonna paint the walls...green." Now that's quality TV.

Starla became enthralled with the drama, so I decided to throw out some rapid-fire questions to test her multitasking prowess. "Hey, Hon, what was the name of Kirk's first dog, and how many stamps do we have? Can you eat a whole Cornish hen in one sitting? Where is Chase's baseball glove? Do we have a wok? Do you know how to make a coconut cream pie?"

Without losing her focus on the TV show, she calmly replied, "Kirk's first dog's name was Frisky. We have six stamps. No, I can't eat a whole Cornish hen in one sitting. Chase's baseball glove is on the floor in his closet. The wok is in the bottom left kitchen cabinet, and you can just ask Heidi Klum to make you a coconut cream pie. Jerkwad."

Honey, I Shrunk My Underpants

A few months ago on a warm Saturday morning, I went to the mall with my family. Starla had to buy something for somebody for some reason (no, I wasn't listening when she explained it to me. I was deeply involved in a very important activity—watching *Gilligan's Island*). I agreed to go with her because she promised we could go to Chick-fil-A after she finished shopping. Simple things make me happy…especially a big ol' barrel of waffle fries.

While she went off to shop, I took the boys to look at the big screen TVs in an electronics store. Oh, how we love to stare at those fabulous creations with the hope that one day Starla will let us take one home.

A 65-inch TV was hooked up to a video camera that captured images of shoppers as they moved through the store. I became very intrigued by one of the unsuspecting patrons caught on camera. The man appeared to be in his early 40s with salt-and-pepper hair, a couple of chins, a cookie belly, and man boobs. He wore a ratty old flannel shirt and sweat pants with a large ketchup stain on the butt (I don't even want to think about how it got there). His butt was so big; it looked like it should be hanging out of the back end of a horse trailer.

Suddenly, two young boys joined the large man on the screen. My highly perceptive seven-year-old son, Chase, said, "Dad, look. We're on TV."

Yep. The pathetic guy with the giant butt was me. Oh, my God, when did this happen? How long have I looked like the "before" picture in a Weight Watchers ad?

When I was younger (translation: before we had kids), I was a gym rat. I worked out six days a week and thought I was in good shape. Like many men, I dreamed of having a buff bod like Sylvester Stallone. Sadly, no one told me that after our first son arrived, everything would change, literally.

For years, I worked long hours at the office and traveled a great deal for consulting engagements. After work, I would go to the gym and burn off the stress of the day. When Chase came along, my daily schedule changed, radically. I put in my 12 hours at work and drove straight home. I desperately wanted to be a great dad and was willing to sacrifice my exercise routine to spend as much time as possible with my family.

The gym became just another building that I drove by on my way home. The manager of the gym categorized me as a "high value customer," which can be more appropriately defined as "fool who pays us every month and never works out."

Within a very short amount of time, my six-pack abs turned into a hairy keg. My classic, muscular V-shape disappeared, and now I look like an H with a thyroid problem. Our home videos should be titled "Buns of Cottage Cheese." My friend Sam calls me the Lord of the Onion Rings. I have to wear Levi's Wide Load jeans.

When I bend over to tie my shoes, I make this bizarre "hhhhuuuuuuugggggh" sound, like reaching over my enormous gut is the most difficult chore on the planet. I even outgrew a belt...a BELT. No one outgrows a stupid belt. I'm so big; Calista Flockhart is in orbit around me.

It seems like every menial task reminds me of how fat I've become. Brushing my teeth has turned into an embarrassing incident. When I vigorously brush my molars, my body shakes like 228 pounds of Jell-O in a paint mixer. The waves of lard rolling over my belly make me seasick. It's disgusting.

One day, while I was getting dressed, I noticed something strange about my underpants. I said to Starla, "Honey, I think my underpants have shrunk." [Insert hysterical laughter here.]

"Don't you think the giant slabs of pecan pie and the mountains of chocolate ice cream you eat at 10:30 every night could be contributing to your situation?"

"Noooooooo, I think you left them in the dryer too long and they shrank. I'm sure that's the problem." (Deny, deny, deny)

"Dream on, waffle fry boy."

That afternoon, I went to Macy's to buy a new fleet of underpants. I was appalled to see that their definition of sizes did not come close to my expectations. I think of myself as a medium—bigger than some guys, smaller than others. Their definition of medium is the perfect fit for a skinny 12-year-old boy. Who makes these size decisions, Lara Flynn Boyle? The large category should be called "underpants for men in their early 20s who still have a metabolism."

I finally came to the realization I would have to settle for the extra large underpants. It's awfully disturbing when the fine print on the package says, "May also be used to sail a 28-foot boat."

Because white clothing gives the illusion of additional weight, I chose the slimming dark blue shades, which were labeled "fashion briefs" (marketing slogan: sumo wrestlers love 'em). Like wearing a pair of dark blue underpants will make any difference when your rear end is approximately the size of Connecticut. Who the heck do I think I'm kidding?

I took my new underpant armada home and made the major mistake of leaving them unguarded on my bed. I was going to put them in a secret hiding place, but I was distracted by a Victoria's Secret commercial, and my brain was unavailable for about 20 minutes.

During this period of temporary fascination, Chase discovered the new additions to my wardrobe. "Wow, Dad, your underpants are huge! Can we use them to make a tent in the backyard?"

My smart-alecky wife chimed in, "Or we could make a hot air balloon and sell tickets for rides at the school carnival. We'll call it Underpants Across America."

"Ha, ha, very funny, but they're not underpants. They're fashion briefs."

"Honey, there is nothing brief about those things."

"Fine. You guys win. I'll go to the gym…tomorrow." And on my way home, I'm gonna stop at Chick-fil-A for a big honkin' bucket o' waffle fries.

Stinkerhead

As the old saying goes, sticks and stones may break my bones but words will crush my self-confidence, leave me with lingering doubts about my value as a human being, and force me to consume massive amounts of Prozac, Paxil, and Zoloft.

Kids can be extremely cruel, and name-calling provides them with an easy way to drive a neurotic child to tears. When I was young, I was the kid who wound masking tape around the middle of my glasses to keep them from splitting apart. Math came easy to me, but talking to girls didn't. In high school, I drove my parents' 1976 Dodge Dart Swinger to football games. Talk about a babe repellant. To put it mildly, I was a supergeek. The other kids called me names like Nerd, Dweeb, Poindexter, and Spaz.

My biggest tormentor was Greg Stafford. Greg was the coolest kid in school. He had perfect hair, perfect teeth, and a smokin' Camero. People followed him everywhere he went as if he was a movie star. He dated Janine Crawford, the hottest girl in the history of the school. Every day of my high school career, Greg called me names like Doofus, Zitface, and Four-Eyed Goon. He pushed me around in the hall, squirted ketchup on my shirt, and gave me atomic wedgies on a regular basis. I hated that guy.

Sure, Greg hurt my feelings, but that was a long time ago. I have matured to the point where I'm no longer bitter about Greg's torture or his insults. Well, OK, maybe I'm still just a little bitter. All right, yes, I'm still angry at that self-centered pretty boy. I hope he lost all of his perfect hair and grew six giant hairy moles on his forehead. I hope Janine dumped him and then ran off to Borneo with an orthodontist named Sheldon. I hope Greg lives miserably with his parents, eating potted meat for every meal while he watches *Wheel of Fortune* reruns with his Aunt Matilda and scratches his head because he's too stupid to figure out the simplest puzzles. I hope he's trapped in a dead-end job with a nerdy boss who persecutes him every freakin' day. I hope he had to ask a geek to fix his computer that crashed because he caught a virus when he was downloading porn off the Internet. I hope he doesn't find out about this book because if he does, he'll probably kidnap me from my home in the middle of the night, take me to my high school, and shove my head in a toilet for old time's sake.

My kids constantly call each other names, and I have to serve as referee. All day long it's, "Dad, Logan called me a butthead," or "Dad, Chase called me a boogerbrain." I keep telling myself they'll grow out of this infuriating phase. I also keep telling myself that one day I'll win the lottery—which hasn't happened yet either.

What if humans didn't evolve past this silly phase and name-calling persisted in our adult lives? You would hear television interviews like this:

Dan Rather: "Good evening, I'm Dan Rather with a very special edition of *48 Hours*. Tonight, I'm speaking with United States Secretary of State Colin Powell. As the war on terrorism drags on, for many of our leaders, the battle becomes a personal struggle to protect America from evil terrorist thugs. Mr. Secretary, what is your personal feeling toward Osama Bin Laden?"

Secretary of State Colin Powell: "Well, Dan, you know I don't usually discuss my personal opinions of individuals; however, in the case of Osama Bin Laden, I'd have to say I think he's a stinkerhead."

Or how would a presidential debate sound? Oh my, the name-calling that could arise between two fiery candidates caught in the heat of competition:

Moderator Chris Mathews: "Vice President Cornblatt, do you support the Republican notion of dramatically cutting taxes to spur the economy?"

Vice President Cornblatt: "Yes, Chris, I believe we can find a way to get our economy back on track with an influx of billions of dollars into the hands of hard working Americans."

Moderator Chris Mathews: "Senator Sneezencrantz, what is your response?"

Senator Sneezencrantz: "Chris, the vice president is a dorkwad."

Vice President Cornblatt: "Oh yeah, well you're a skirt-chasing, money-grubbing, left wingnut who couldn't find his butt with both hands."

Senator Sneezencrantz: "Am not."

Vice President Cornblatt: "Are too."

Senator Sneezencrantz: "Am not."

Vice President Cornblatt: "Are too."

Moderator Chris Mathews: "That's enough. Our country is doomed if you chuckleheads are the best presidential candidates we can find. Our time is up. Join me next week for a debate between Minnesota Senator Alan Flingtone and California Senator John Robertsketterer. Our subject will be…my governor can beat up your governor."

Wouldn't you love to be in a business meeting and say exactly what you were really thinking? Let's say you're in a conference room with six of your coworkers and your boss, Mr. Dinglehopper.

Mr. Dinglehopper: "Today I'd like to discuss a new cost reduction idea that has been submitted by Bob Weezengruber. Bob, can you please present your idea to the team?"

Bob Weezengruber: "Yes, thank you, Mr. Dinglehopper. In an effort to cut our costs and bring the company back to profitability, I believe we each should take a voluntary salary reduction of at least 35%, pay for our own health insurance, decline our annual stock option allotment, and pay $50 a week for the use of our coffee machine."

Mr. Dinglehopper: "Well, team…what do you think about Bob's idea?"

You: "I think Bob is a weinerhead. To punish him for conjuring up this lame idea, we should make him stand at the reception desk in the lobby wearing nothing but a zebra-skin thong and sing Barry Manilow songs all afternoon."

Mr. Dinglehopper: "Sounds good to me. All in favor…"

The Team: "Aye. Aye. Aye. Aye. Nay. Aye. Aye."

Mr. Dinglehopper: "The Ayes have it. OK, Bob, get out of your cheap suit and start singing."

Bob Weezengruber: "Her name was Lola…"

One night after a particularly brutal name-calling session, I sat the boys down at the kitchen table. "Guys, you have to stop calling each other names. I don't want to hear that kind of language anymore from either one of you. You are making me crazy."

Logan pleaded his case, "Chase started it."

"I did not. You're a stinkpot."

"Daddy, Chase called me a stinkpot."

The doorbell interrupted this riveting conversation. "Starla, can you get the door? I'm trying to have a serious discussion with the boys." *And failing miserably.*

Starla called from the doorway, "Some guy wants to talk to you."

"Who is it?" I asked.

"He says his name is Greg Stafford."

The School Field Trip

One day last April, Chase brought a note home from school announcing a field trip to see a show at a local college. The note asked parents to serve as chaperones for the outing, which would take place the following Tuesday morning. "You should volunteer," Starla suggested.

"Can't. I have to work."

"You write silly stories about farts. I think you can make time in your busy schedule to go with your son on a field trip. Andrew's mom is going to chaperone, so you'll have someone to help you." Writer's note: Andrew's mom is very good looking.

"OK, I'll go."

Tuesday morning, we arrived at Chase's class promptly at 9:00 AM. I tried to score brownie points with his teacher, Mrs. Haggerty. "Hi. We're here and ready to have all kinds of fun!"

"You were supposed to be here at 8:30." *Oops.* "Today, you will be responsible for the safety of your son, Chase, and three additional children: Chuckie Manson, A. Davis Wadsworth III, and Fabiola."

I looked around the room for the three kids. "Where are they?"

"All of the kids are on the bus, except Chuckie. You need to find him," Mrs. Haggerty said in a tone that only teachers know how to use.

I turned to Chase and said, "Help me find Chuckie." He pointed to a desk in the back of the room. I could hear someone whispering. I peered under the desk and discovered a disheveled kid talking to himself. "You must be Chuckie. Go get on the bus."

As we walked out of the school, Chase quietly gave me the lowdown on Chuckie. "He wants to be a musician, and he really likes some old guys called the Beach Boys. One day he's gonna have a big family." Chuckie had long, greasy hair and psycho eyes. He wore a tee shirt that said, "Roses are red, violets are blue, I hate kittens, and I hate you too." What a delightful child.

"Do me a favor. Stay away from Chuckie."

"No problem, Dad. He's a nutcase." *My thoughts exactly.*

We boarded the bus and I looked for the other two kids. I discovered them sitting together in the back seat. I introduced myself, "Hi. You must be Davis and Fabiola. I'm Chase's dad, Mr. Alderman, and I'll be your chaperone today."

"My name is A. Davis Wadsworth III." He was wearing a tailored gray pinstripe suit with a white shirt and a yellow power bowtie.

"It's nice to meet you, Davis."

"As I mentioned previously, my name is A. Davis Wadsworth III. You will kindly use my entire name when you address me." *Now I know what the "A" stands for.*

I shifted my focus to the girl sitting next to him. "And you must be Fabiola. What's your last name?"

"I don't have a last name. I am a diva. Divas do not have last names. You know…Cher…Madonna…Fabiola." She snapped her fingers in a "Z" and flicked her long blonde hair over her shoulder.

My son said, "Her real name is Hannah Tyler. She's a singer. She auditioned for *America's Most Talented Kid*, but she lost to a guy who could burp the national anthem."

I looked at my son and winked. "She's kinda cute."

"Too high maintenance for me," he said. *Where did he hear that?*

I surveyed the bus for Andrew's mom. No sign of her. I found Mrs. Haggerty and asked, "Where is Andrew's mom? Isn't she supposed to be here?"

"She just called. She's not feeling well today. Looks like it's just you and me…and 18 first graders." My stomach felt like a volcano that was about to erupt—Mount Blowachunka. I staggered to the back of the bus and sat with Chase in front of Fabiola and Davis. Excuse me…A. Davis Wadsworth III.

"Why aren't you at work today?" A. Davis Wadsworth III asked.

"Because I wanted to have some fun with my son, Chase."

"Judging by your cheap jeans and golf shirt, I can surmise that you don't have a real job. My father is a partner with BearingPoint. He has a very important position and makes lots of money. He graduated from Princeton University."

Chase came to my rescue. "My dad writes funny stories about farts."

Two additional classes joined us on the bus. The vehicle was jam-packed with 68 first graders, all missing at least one tooth. It was like traveling with a team of short, skinny hockey players. As we drove down the highway, my ears began ringing because the noise level was far beyond the threshold of pain. I felt like I had stuck my head inside a jet engine. I had no idea 68 children could make more noise than Metallica.

We arrived at the college auditorium and unloaded the snaggletooth bunch. Mrs. Haggerty told the kids to make a straight line and walk quietly. To my surprise, they followed her directions perfectly. How did she do that? The kids marched to their seats. Mrs. Haggerty asked if anyone had to go to the bathroom. Nope. Not one kid. They were ready for the show.

The production was vaguely familiar. It was called *Juanita White and the Seven Vertically Challenged Men*. This politically correct story was about a beautiful multi-cultural woman who lived with seven undersized mine workers. I think they met at the craps tables at the MGM Grand Hotel in Las Vegas. They had a few drinks, one thing led to another, and they decided to share a five bedroom home near the mine. This kind of thing happens every day.

Each of the seven diminutive men had an unusual personal history. Doc was an OB-GYN who left medicine because he couldn't afford the malpractice insurance premiums. Bashful never missed an episode of *Will & Grace*. Stinky had a brutal case of body odor. Grumpy suffered with a bipolar disorder. H. Ross wanted to be President of the United States. Dopey escaped from the Betty Ford Clinic, and Happy was addicted to Viagra.

Fifteen minutes into the show, A. Davis Wadsworth III informed me of his intense need to go to the bathroom. This event started a chain reaction of bathroom visits that spanned the rest of the show. I missed most of the good parts, but luckily I was able to see the final scene where Juanita dumped Prince Charming and ran off to ski in Vail, Colorado with Happy.

After the show, Mrs. Haggerty and I shepherded the flock back to the bus. On the ride home, I realized the bus did not have seat belts. According to the law, to ride in a car, a child has to be strapped into a car seat with a five point restraint system using seat belts, duct tape, bailing twine, and chicken wire. But on a bus, a giant hunk of metal with thinly padded seats, children can sit three to a seat and bounce around like rubber balls while the vehicle travels at speeds of over 60 MPH. Can someone explain this to me?

We arrived at the school and the kids quickly returned to their classroom. Mrs. Haggerty gave the students a math worksheet to complete. Heads down, pencils flying, they quickly found their learning groove. I admired Mrs. Haggerty's ability to work with the children. My respect for teachers grew exponentially on that Tuesday morning.

"What are you going to do the rest of the day?" I asked.

"We'll work on math, reading, and history for a while. Then we'll go to the computer lab. How about you? What are you going to do this afternoon?" she asked.

"I'm gonna write a funny story about farts."

I'm a Fashion Disaster

I'm not what you would call a slave to fashion. As a teenager in the '70s, I actually wore a powder blue leisure suit with two-inch platform shoes. I looked bad. No, not the good "bad" as in the way Laurence Fishburne looked "bad" as Morpheus in the Matrix. I mean bad as in, "Oh, my God, I can't believe I actually went out in public looking like that. What the heck was I thinking?" I didn't look cool back then and I don't look cool now.

Starla says my sense of style is derived from the Garanimal theory of mix-and-match clothing. You can wear almost anything with blue jeans, and any color shirt can be worn with beige khakis. Easy, right?

I don't shop at expensive men's stores because it doesn't make sense to me to put a $200 shirt on a $24 body. Like many men, I wait for the Dockers half-price sale at Macy's, and then I buy eight pairs of pants, which I wear until they develop holes in unsightly places.

I've resigned myself to the fact that I will never be on the cover of *GQ*, and I don't have a chance to ever be considered for *People Magazine's 50 Most Beautiful People Issue*. I do believe, however, that I have a pretty good shot to be featured as one of *Field & Stream's 50 Most Ordinary Looking Men with Ugly Feet and Excessive Ear Wax*.

The media is infested with fashion gurus who tell us how to take advantage of the latest trends so we can look hip when we go out to fabulous dinner parties. On television, fashion critics analyze pictures of celebrities and berate them on the clothes they wear. Frankly, I don't care what blouse Jennifer Aniston wore last Tuesday to fill her car up with gas or what dress Sharon Stone wore Saturday morning when she was shopping for stewed tomatoes at Safeway. What amazes me is the fact that some of the fashion critics wear the most hideous clothes I have ever seen. One day I saw a fashion "expert" on the *Today* show wearing an orange paisley shirt, a wide white belt, and lime green pants. He looked like my Uncle Lou who lives in a retirement community in Boca Raton, cheats at checkers, and eats mashed potatoes for every meal because his wobbly dentures make it impossible for him to bite through a piece of chicken. Evidently, Uncle Lou is very in-touch with the unpredictable whims of the fashion industry. He probably has lunch with Donatella Versace every Thursday at Morrison's Cafeteria to compare ideas on hemlines and open toe shoes. Who knew?

When I was a kid in the '60s, parents herded their young boys into ancient barbershops and paid two bucks to have their boys' heads shaved. It wasn't a fashion statement by any means. It was a low maintenance way for parents to keep their kids from looking like those heathen hippies who made such a ruckus at Woodstock. The kids looked like seven-year-old Marines and hated it. Now parents take their kids to Cartoon Cuts and pay $29 for the same haircut. The kids love it because they look like some untalented rapper who has a buzz cut.

Another hair style I don't understand is the bed head look. *American Idol* host Ryan Seacrest and second banana Clay Aiken popularized this trend to a point where millions of kids spend hours lathering their heads with gels and using flat irons to make their hair look like they just rolled out of the sack. I don't even iron my shirts, why in the heck would people want to take the time to iron their hair to make it look like they just woke up? I say to you young people all over the world…stop the insanity. Do something useful with your life. Comb your hair.

Throughout my childhood, my mother told me at least 10 times a day to tuck in my shirt. It was an obsession for her. No matter where I was or what I was doing, my shirt had to be tucked tightly into my pants. If by chance my shirt happened to be in a disheveled state of untuckedness, she would say, "If you don't tuck in your shirt right now, I'm gonna jerk a knot in your tail." I never knew exactly what this old Southern expression meant, but I sure as heck didn't want to find out. The other day I saw actor Will Smith (fashion icon and star of many blockbuster movies including *Men in Black* and *Independence Day*) on television standing in plain sight in front of God and everybody with…[Gasp]…his shirt hanging loosely OUTSIDE OF HIS PANTS. What is going on here? Did I miss a memo? When did this untucking activity become socially acceptable? Does his mother know he violated the sacred shirt tucking directive on national television? I bet she jerked a knot in his tail when he got home.

My biggest fashion-based pet peeve is the mishandling of baseball caps. For a few years now, I've seen kids all over the United States wearing their baseball caps in an improper fashion, and it must stop right now. They wear their hats backward or cocked sideways. I've even seen some kids wear golf visors sideways and UPSIDE DOWN. I had no idea it was this difficult to operate a hat. It seems like a simple task to master.

There are a very few guys who can actually look good wearing their baseball hat backwards. Ken Griffey Jr. can get away with it because he has one of the most perfect swings in the history of baseball and looks ubercool no matter how he wears his hat. I don't care if he has been hurt a lot; Jr. is still one of the greatest players of all time and always looks stylish—even with his hat on backwards. Mel Gibson can wear his baseball hat backwards because…well, duh…he's Mel Gibson. Donald Trump can wear his hat any way he wants to because he is a gazillionaire and should do anything he can to cover up his incredibly bad haircut.

If you are not Ken Griffey Jr., Mel Gibson, or Donald Trump, please wear your baseball cap correctly. If you comply with my request, I promise you will look 100% better. Middle-aged men will respect you. Women will…um…women will always wish that you were Mel Gibson. Sorry, but it's the truth, and there's nothing you can do about that.

In closing, I want to direct my final statement to every young American male who thinks it's cool to wear a baseball cap the wrong way. Let me be crystal clear about this: the front of your hat goes on the front of your head. If you continue to operate your hat in an inappropriate manner, I'm gonna jerk a knot in your tail.

I'll Have the Prime Rib With a Side Order of Valium

I have tried to teach my boys the fine art of dining in a nice restaurant. So far, they have learned one important fact: fancy ketchup packets explode when you smack them on your brother's forehead.

Every time we go out to eat, I think to myself, "This time, they will behave like civilized human beings in the restaurant." What a ludicrous thought. It's like saying, "This time, Gilligan will find a way to get off the island."

One Friday night, we decided to make another gallant attempt to take the boys out to dinner. Trouble started as soon as we got in the car. "Dad, can we get ice cream?" They both whined before their seat belts were fastened. I explained the importance of eating a well-balanced meal before dessert, which they ignored as they munched on Doritos that had been lodged in the back seat for more than six years.

Our restaurant of choice was Logan's Roadhouse, which for obvious reasons is my son Logan's favorite place to eat. Logan's Roadhouse is a great place to take the kids because you get to eat peanuts and throw the shells on the floor. It is a perfect location for the boys to unleash their carnage. How much damage could they do in a place like this? I wish I hadn't said that.

As we walked into the restaurant, Starla said, "There's a line."

Unfortunately, I left my spousal language translator in my other pants. This phrase actually translates into "There's a line, and if we wait, the boys will humiliate me in front of 20 people I don't know, so let's get back in the car and go somewhere else, you chucklehead."

"The line moves fast here. We'll be fine." *Oh, you stupid, stupid man.*

As we waited, Logan sang "It's a Small World After All" over and over at the top of his lungs. Chase couldn't stop talking. "Dad, do you think the man in front of us is married to the girl that looks like his daughter? They were kissing, but not on the cheek like we kiss Mom. They were kissing sloppy like the people on TV. That's so gross."

"You watch too much TV. Knock it off."

"Dad, that lady over there is very large. Do you think she weighs more than our car? I bet she could eat a whole cow."

Starla looked at me and gave me her sarcastic smile that means, "If I were a mean person, I would lace a chuckwagon steak with arsenic and bury your body where no one would ever find it."

I couldn't get that darned song "It's a Small World After All" out of my head. It's like an evil mind control mechanism that took over my brain. Please make it stop!

"Your table is ready," said Jane, our perky hostess. Thank goodness. We walked to our table, crunching peanut shells along the way. The hostess seated us between an elderly couple on one side and a family with two young girls in an adjoining booth. The boys dove into a bucket of peanuts.

I made the mistake of looking at the menu for three seconds. When I looked up, Logan was gently placing peanut shells in the elderly man's toupee. Luckily, the man couldn't feel them because his rug was as thick as a beaver pelt.

Our waiter, Brandon, brought the boys coloring books and crayons. "Can I get you something to drink?" he asked.

"Grape juice gives me diarrhea," Logan blurted.

"Thanks for sharing, Buddy. He'll have milk," I said.

The kids focused their attention on the new coloring books. Unfortunately, Brandon, a 19-year-old college student, did not know that it is imperative to give two brothers the same colors of crayons. This was a disaster. Chase got blue and red. Logan had green and yellow. "I want the blue one," Logan screamed. He snatched the blue crayon from Chase, which, of course, started a fight.

Brandon returned with our drinks to see that I had Chase subdued with a headlock and that Starla had Logan in the sleeper hold. "Could you please bring us four more crayons—exactly like the first four?" I asked, as I clamped down on Chase to keep him from leaping across the table.

The young waiter tilted his head sideways and looked like a cocker spaniel staring at a math problem. "Uh…okay." He walked away shaking his head.

He fetched the crayons and we placed our orders. "I'll have the prime rib with a side order of Valium and a nice steaming hot cup of Prozac," I said straight-faced.

"Dude, I think we're out of Valium, but I'll check." Poor Brandon wasn't the sharpest knife in the drawer. He ambled to the kitchen trying to figure out how to spell Prozac.

While the boys were coloring, I turned my head to admire the beautiful accoutrements adorning the establishment. When I looked back, the boys were swinging from the light fixture, and throwing lemon slices at the nice family in the next booth. Good Lord, it's like we were dining with two young orangutans that had just escaped from the National Zoo.

"I'm terribly sorry," Starla said to the mom. Her girls were sitting quietly like two little angels, while my guys were wreaking havoc like two weapons of mass destruction. She looked at my wife with a pitiful expression as if to say, "I'm so sorry you have to live with those testosterone-impaired heathens."

Logan stood up on his chair and stared into space with a strained look on his face. "What's the matter?" Starla asked.

"I HAVE TO POOP," he announced. As Starla escorted him to the bathroom, he told every person he met along the way of his intentions. "I gotta poop." "Hey, Mister, I'm gonna go poop." "I'm on my way to the poop factory."

After he completed his task, he marched through the crowd receiving congratulatory high-fives. Life is good when you're a three-year-old.

Brandon delivered our food and we dug into our entrées. Logan took one bite of a chicken tender. "I'm done," he declared. I expected this to happen, so I was fully prepared to finish the rest of his meal. That's what dads do.

He jumped down from his chair and made a beeline to the elderly lady in the next booth. "Can I see your belly button?" Logan asked. Starla was mortified.

I came to the rescue. "I have a better idea, Buddy. Why don't you go ask that blonde girl if you can see her belly button? Come on, I'll go with you."

"I don't think so, Mister," Starla stated in her "you are so busted" tone.

We wolfed down dinner, corralled the boys, and hurried out of the restaurant before they violated a health code. As we were leaving, we saw a doctor who works with Starla at an outpatient surgery center. He was standing in line with his wife and three sons, ages three, six, and eight.

This doctor is the kind of guy who brags incessantly about how he sold his Internet stocks in early 2000…and he just bought a new BMW…and his wife is a lingerie model. In other words, he's a weinerhead and I can't stand him.

He called me over to tell me about a new sailboat he just purchased. I pretended to listen for a bit, and then I leaned down to talk to his three-year-old. "Hi there, Champ. Hey, I have an idea for you. While you're waiting in line, why don't you sing a song? How about "It's a Small World After All?" I'm sure your dad will love that song!"

Dad, Can I Ask You a Question?

I'm not a complete idiot. I graduated in the top 80% of my class at Virginia Tech. I know lots of important junk such as...Jack Jones sang the *Love Boat* theme song from 1977 to 1985 and then Dionne Warwick sang the theme song in the final season of the show, Willie Mays hit 660 home runs, and rocker Alice Cooper's real name is Vincent Furnier. This information didn't help me on the SATs, but I'm a whiz at Trivial Pursuit. My mother is so proud of me.

Smart people are very popular these days. I am particularly amazed at the investigators on the *CSI* television show. Those people know everything. (All right, yes, I like the hot redhead Marg Helgenberger—but she's smart too.) The other night, the CSI team investigated the case of a man who was murdered in a parked car. Marg found a Chicklet on the passenger seat. She picked up the tiny piece of gum with a pair of tweezers and said, "This is a Wrigley's Apple Flavored Chicklet. It is produced in Germany. The ingredients include maltitol, sorbitol, mannitol, aspartame gum base, glycerol, gum arabic, titanium dioxide, lecithin, carnauba wax, and butylated hydroxyanisole. It's also considered to be a source of phenylalanine."

"How do you know so much about Chicklets?" a young CSI trainee asked.

"I do my homework, kid. A little reading goes a long way," Marg replied.

"How could a Chicklet be involved in this murder?"

Marg slipped on a pair of dark sunglasses and said, "Tough to say at this point. We'll uncover the details when we analyze the Chicklet back in the crime lab."

The trainee yearned for more insight into the case and asked, "What do you think happened here? What does your gut tell you?"

Marg smiled wisely and said, "I don't listen to my gut. I listen to the evidence." Now that's an intelligent person talking right there, and she looked incredible in her low-cut blouse and skin-tight Levi's. Smart is sexy.

My boys are still young enough to think I'm a genius. I'm sure this will come to a screeching halt when they turn 13, but for now they look to me for information. Every day my kids ask me a bazillion questions. Unfortunately, I can answer only approximately 16% of the questions correctly. The rest of the time, I have to make up wild guesses. At some point in the near future, they'll realize I'm giving them bogus data and find the answers to all of their questions with Google.

As my gift to dads around the world, I have compiled a list of actual questions my boys have asked me and my respective answers to said questions. If you are confronted with these same questions, please feel free to use these answers.

Child's Question	Your Answer
Who invented the pencil?	N. J. Conte invented the pencil in 1795. His first attempt, the No. 1 model, didn't work very well, but his second attempt, the No. 2 pencil, was a big success.
How old is Mommy?	Twenty-eight. No matter how old Mommy really is, your answer should always be 28. Just trust me on this one.
If I say Megan is my girlfriend, will she get a baby in her belly?	Ask your mother and stay away from Megan.
What is God's last name?	Harold…as in "Hark the Harold angels sing."
Why do zebras have stripes?	To make them look thinner.
If I can't say a bad word out loud, can I whisper it like you do, Daddy?	Yes, but only if Mommy is not within a 10-mile radius.
Were the dinosaurs really killed by a big meteorite?	No. They had high cholesterol and were nagged to death by their doctors.
Does the Green Lantern ever go to the bathroom?	Yes. His poop is emerald green and glows in the dark.
Do dogs like to watch TV?	Yes, but they're sick of reality shows.
When you flush a dead goldfish down the toilet, where does the fish go?	Des Moines, Iowa.

Many questions have remained unanswered for years. Why are we here? What is the true meaning of life? What's love got to do with it? These ethereal questions will probably never be answered. Although I try not to ponder such complicated topics, I do have a few questions of my own:

- Is it OK for a chunky, 40-something white guy to feel bootylicious? Oh, how I hope it's acceptable, because if feeling bootylicious is wrong, I don't wanna be right.

- Why does Yogi Bear wear a tie?

- Why do I keep getting e-mails from people who say they have technology that can enlarge my organ in just a matter of days? How and why did they get my name? I happen to be quite pleased with the size of my Wurlitzer, and I wish those people would just leave me alone.

- Does anybody really know what time it is?

- What was Bullwinkle's major at Wassamatta U.? I'm guessing art history.

- How come movie stars say they don't care about money and then they force the film studios to pay them $20 million plus a percentage of the box office for a lousy movie? They claim, "It's not about the money; it's about practicing my craft." Just once I'd like to hear a regular guy named Dave say, "I don't fix lawn mowers for the money; it's my way of paying homage to my craft."

- The Psychic Friends Network went bankrupt. Shouldn't they have seen that coming?

- Why are so many beautiful women attracted to ugly guys? Here are some examples: Pamela Anderson and Kid Rock, Shania Twain and Robert "Mutt" Lange, Paulina Porizkova and Ric Ocasek, Christy Brinkley and Billy Joel, Kate Hudson and Chris Robinson, Starla and me…hmmm…disregard this question. Let's move on.

- If a cat actually got your tongue, what do you think he would do with it?

- If a rabbit took a Viagra, would he explode?

Children learn by asking questions, so we should encourage them to be inquisitive and curious. When your child asks a difficult question, provide your answer with excitement and support. Don't be afraid to say, "I don't know; let's look it up on the Internet together," and most of all, don't feel insecure about the size of your Wurlitzer.

I'm Bored

Chase completed his first grade school year on a beautiful Friday in June. Over the following weekend, he attended three birthday parties and a super soaker bash at his friend Taylor's house.

On Monday at 7:00 AM, he began his noble quest to have the perfect summer vacation. After he shoveled down a gigantic bowl of Cocoa Puffs, I sent him into the family room for an early round of cartoons and made my 10-second commute to work in my home office.

By 7:30 AM, I was pounding away at my computer, researching the latest developments in Oracle's attempt to take over PeopleSoft and gain superiority in the enterprise software industry. Well…um…that's not exactly true. Actually, I was reading a research paper on the plight of the Tasmanian Tiger, a large dog-like Australian marsupial that became extinct in the '30s. Uh…that's not completely accurate. I was surfing through Jillian Barberie's website at www.jillian-sworld.com. Jillian is a co-host of the pseudo-news show *Good Day Live* and the sexy weather girl on *Fox NFL Sunday*. I happen to find Jillian's advice on moisturizing creams to be quite insightful and informative. That's another lie…I was looking at pictures from Jillian's photo shoot for *Maxim Magazine*. So, sue me.

At 7:45 AM, Chase walked into my office and said, "I'm bored."

"You've been on summer vacation for only 45 minutes. How can you possibly be bored already? Why don't you watch some cartoons?"

"They're reruns."

"You could play on your computer."

"Don't wanna."

"You could do some math exercises. You're very good at math." He looked at me like I had a rutabaga growing out of my skull. He moped back into the family room and rummaged through his toy box to find something remotely interesting. We tried snacks, Legos, board games, DVDs, and his Hot Wheels racetrack. No luck—still bored. Every 20 minutes for the rest of the day, he drifted into my office and sulked. I didn't get a lick of work done, and I never got a chance to see Jillian Barberie's pictures with Carmen Electra. Something had to be done about this situation.

"Tomorrow, I'll take the day off and we'll do something really fun."

"What are we gonna do?" Chase asked.

"I dunno, but I'll think of something by tomorrow morning." Oops. I had committed to a day of fun without planning any activities, which could be a problem.

When Starla came home from work, I explained my precarious predicament to her. She immediately said, "Why don't you go to the Smithsonian Institution and see the dinosaur skeletons. Chase would have fun, and it takes less than an hour to get there." My wife is a genius and she has strong arm muscles (she made me write that).

I called Chase into my office. "I have a great idea. How would you like to go to the Smithsonian Institution and see some dinosaur skeletons?"

"Yeah, cool. It was Mom's idea, right?" Sometimes he's a little too bright for his young age.

Tuesday morning we got up early and headed out on our summer field trip. Because we live in the Northern Virginia suburbs, just outside of Washington, D.C., we could easily jump on the mass transit Metrorail system and get off at a Metro stop situated in the middle of the Smithsonian buildings. The Metro train buzzed with government workers, corporate professionals, and a guy that smelled like garlic who chose to sit behind us and ooze his stench for the entire 50-minute ride.

We arrived at the Smithsonian's National Museum of Natural History when it opened at 10:00 AM and ran straight to the dinosaur exhibit. Chase marveled at the sheer size of the tyrannosaurus rex and the brontosaurus. We took pictures of monsters such as the triceratops, stegosaurus and the pterodactyl. Chase became intrigued by a giant sloth, a creature the size of an elephant that lived during the Ice Age. Some paleontologists believe the giant sloth evolved into a lumpy guy named Ernie Offenbacker who works part time at the post office in Beulah, North Dakota.

I had no idea there were so many different kinds of dinosaurs. Everyone knows about the T-Rex and raptors, which were popularized by the Jurassic Park films. But not many people have heard about the more obscure dinosaurs that have not received a great deal of media attention. For example, have you ever heard of the elusive JenniferLopezasaurus? This stunning female dinosaur mesmerized male dinosaurs with her exquisite round tail. Although she had brief relationships with several male dinos, her one true love was the BenAffleckatops. To this day, scientists have not been able to determine how long their relationship actually lasted.

The most mysterious dinosaur is the fabled JimmyHoffasaurus. For countless years, paleontologists have searched for the remains of a JimmyHoffasaurus, but to date, no one has been able to determine what happened to him. Various scientists believe he became extinct in a garden-like area that later became known as Detroit. Some people (when I say some people, I mean people who are not me) say the JimmyHoffasaurus was whacked by a Maffiapod and sent to swim with the prehistoric fishies. I have no opinion whatsoever on the whereabouts of the remains of the JimmyHoffasaurus or the activities of the Maffiapod family. We'll probably never know the true story of his extinction.

The coolest dinosaur was, by far, the Shaftasaurus. This powerful dino had a shiny black leather coat and walked through the forest with a style no other creature could match. He was a complicated dino and no one understood him but his mate. Not even the T-Rex would mess with him because the Shaftasaurus was a bad mother…[Shut your mouth]…but I'm just talkin' about the Shaftasaurus. Can you dig it?

After we made our rounds through the dinosaur skeletons, Chase and I wandered through an ancient sea display featuring a giant squid and an insect zoo that included a presentation of a hairy tarantula. We capped our day with an exciting 3-D IMAX movie about a T-Rex.

After a crowded Metro ride home and a big dinner, Chase fell asleep on the couch at 7:00 PM—two hours ahead of his normal bedtime. I kissed him on the forehead and carried him upstairs to his room. I felt good knowing we had a great father and son day together.

Wednesday, I started my work day at 7:30 AM sharp. Ten minutes later, Chase meandered into my office. "I had fun with you yesterday, Chase. Did you have a good time at the museum?"

"Yeah, it was way cool. I liked the giant sloth and the 3-D movie."

"What can I do for you this morning, Buddy?"

"I'm bored."

The Birds and the Bees

One morning, as I conducted my daily literary exploration (nonprofessional writers often refer to this activity as "reading the newspaper"), I came upon a story that threw me into a state of shock. Evidently, some kids are starting to "date" at a very young age now. By young, I don't mean 13 or 14; I mean eight...yes, eight years old...as in only a year older than Chase. I feel woozy.

Precocious children throughout the country are beginning to court each other by going to McDonald's for a Happy Meal and then taking in a movie like *Finding Nemo*. Boys are presenting their dates with flowers, and girls are spending hours getting ready so they can look just right for their eight-year-old suitors. I can't believe their parents are supporting this kind of behavior. An eight-year-old boy should be concerned with guy stuff like making slingshots and collecting baseball cards, not slapping on a handful of Hi Karate, blasting his mouth full of Binaca, and complimenting an eight-year-old girl on her new Hello Kitty watch. This is just plain wrong.

In some social circles, girls are now initiating the process by asking boys to take them out for a night on the town. When did this planetary shift occur? Where was I when this happened? Buying socks at Target? Throughout my teenage years, the standard dating process went like this: I saw the prettiest girl in my class, Charlene Owens, standing at her locker at school, and I casually sauntered over to her. I was sure I would impress her with my new Lynyrd Skynyrd tee shirt. I started the conversation off with a smooth line. "Hi, Charlene, how did you do on Mr. Engoian's history test?"

"Who are you?"

"I'm Dale...Alderman. We've been in school together since kindergarten. I sit next to you in third period history class. Remember me?"

"No."

"OK, well, um...I was just wondering if you would like to go out with me on Friday night. We could go to Long John Silver's for dinner and then go see *Smokey and the Bandit*." Hey, give me a break. It was 1977 and I was only 16 years old.

"So, let me get this straight. You want ME to go on a date...with YOU?"

"Yes." The anticipation nearly killed me as Charlene paused to collect her thoughts.

"Listen to me very carefully, loser. Get your zit-covered face away from me and never, I mean, NEVER attempt to talk to me again. Is that clear?"

"So, what are you saying Charlene?"

"No. I will not go out with you. You're repulsive. You're nauseating. You're disgusting. Leave...me...ALONE." Charlene walked out of my life that day and never returned. My dream date crushed my ego. A few years later, I heard she married a fertilizer salesman named J. R. Whorley, had two sets of butt-ugly twins, gained 250 pounds, and lived in a doublewide trailer on the outskirts of Tupelo, Mississippi, next door to her husband's parents. I'm happy for her.

This idea of young kids dating is way too much for me to handle right now. I'm not ready to have the "discussion" with Chase about the birds and the bees. My parents didn't have the discussion with me until I had reached the age of...well, actually, I'm still waiting. I'm very confused about the whole concept of using birds and bees to illustrate the facts of life. Why are they used as examples? If you analyze the actual mating habits of these animals, you would not be so inclined to use them as exemplary models of acceptable dating procedures. According to Anthony Nastase, an Indiana University of Pennsylvania biology professor, birds get around, if you know what I mean. "It's been previously thought that birds were 90% monogamous," Nastase said. "Quite simply, our research is suggesting that is not true."

Peter Dunn, a biologist at the University of Wisconsin–Milwaukee, says the most promiscuous bird in the world is the Australian fairy-wren. About 75% of the wren's offspring are the result of extra-marital affairs, which often occur after a seduction ritual in which a male lures a female away from her mate by bringing her a flower. Numerous male birds have also been sighted frequenting strip clubs with Motley Crue drummer and bad-boy rocker Tommy Lee. You can reach your own conclusions, but birds sound pretty sleazy to me.

Honey bees live in an established colony that includes a single queen (a reproductive female), a few drones (reproductive males), and approximately 80,000 worker bees (non-reproductive females). The queen is the only sexually productive female in the colony and usually mates with six or more drones over the course of a few days. In other words, she's a tramp. Drones are stingless, defenseless cowards. They cannot even feed themselves; they are fed by the worker bees. A drone's only function in life is to mate with a new queen. After mating, which always takes place in the air, a drone dies immediately. It sounds like this, "Yeah baby, yeah"...thud. Worker bees build and maintain the nest and care for the larvae bee babies. These tough workers gather nectar, pollen, and water. They convert the nectar to honey, vacuum the honeycomb, make the beds, clean the toilets, and feed the larvae, the drones, and the queen. In time of danger, the workers defend the colony with their pointy stingers. Worker bees never mate. If you've ever wondered why worker bees seem so mad all of the time, now you know. You'd be mighty angry too if you had to do all of the work around the hive and never had an opportunity to get a little action.

Among the 4,000 species of mammals on Earth, less than 3% are considered to be monogamous including colobus monkeys, mongooses, and snuggle-loving prairie voles. About 40% of men and 30% of women in the United States acknowledge having had at least one extramarital affair, and more than 80% of human societies throughout the world practice some form of polygamy, according to David Barash and Judith Eve Lipton, authors of *The Myth of Monogamy*. So let me make sure I understand this: as a species, mongooses tend to be more loyal to their mates than humans. Oh dear.

When I have "the talk" with Chase, should I use the standard birds and bees illustrations, even though birds sleep around and the queen bee is easy? Or should I go with a dialogue about a loving pair of snuggle-loving prairie voles?

Maybe I'll make up my own story to demonstrate the complexities associated with the facts of life. It will start like this: "Once upon a time, there was an evil witch who tormented teenage boys. Her name was Charlene Owens."

Happy Birthday to Me

Today is my birthday. It's hard for me to believe I'm 42 years old. I remember when I used to think people in their 30s were ancient, and now here I am waiting for my mid-life crisis to arrive. I hope it's a good one that involves a sleek red sports car and fancy Armani suits. Knowing my luck, my mid-life crisis will get lost in the mail and wind up on the doorstep of a guy named Carl who works as a chimney sweep in Mobile, Alabama.

In my mind, on the one hand, I'm still an energetic, 20-something rebel on the prowl for adventure and intrigue. My body, on the other hand, has decided to take a more conservative approach to life and has faded into semi-retirement. When I sit in my big dad chair for a long period of time (defined as anything more than 15 minutes), my joints become stiff. I'm a walking advertisement for Therapeutic Warm Wraps. In just a few short years, I'll probably refuse to drive my car over 40 MPH, wear a fedora, get the gout, and complain incessantly about the government. Come to think of it, I might look good in a fedora. Frank Sinatra looked good in a fedora. Oh crap, it's starting already.

Lately, I have noticed that Muzak has gotten pretty good. No, not just pretty good—Muzak rocks! The other day, I was in the shoe department of a Macy's store and found myself gettin' my groove on to a Muzak version of the classic '70s song, "Brandy," which was made famous by the group Looking Glass. I rocked my rickety ol' rump and sang at the top of my lungs. The hits just kept on coming. "China Grove," "Momma Told Me Not To Come," "Boogie Oogie Oogie," and "Do You Know the Way to San José" filled the air with nostalgia. I grabbed a shoehorn and used it as a microphone to sing my favorite Osmond hit, "One Bad Apple." Ah, the Osmonds—now there's a true supergroup. I had to sit down and compose myself when I heard Wayne Newton's sentimental favorite, "Daddy, Don't You Walk So Fast." That song gets to me every time I think about it. Can somebody please bring me a tissue?

I am what many people refer to as an "older" dad. I was 35 years old when Chase was born and 38 when Logan arrived on the scene. It has become quite common for couples to wait until later in life to have kids, and it worked for us; however, I will admit that being 42 with a three-year-old is no picnic. Logan is built like a linebacker. Picking him up is darned near impossible for me, and carrying him up a flight of stairs is completely out of the question. Unfortunately, I used up my lifetime allowance of patience by August 24, 1993, so living with a rambunctious three-year-old can be maddening for an old fart like me. Do you know how many times a three-year-old can crash a PC in an hour, simply by playing a *Reader Rabbit* computer game? Do you know how fast a three-year-old can run through a crowded mall? Do you have any idea how much it hurts to give a 46-pound boy a piggyback ride on an aching back? Do you know a good chiropractor?

Some people are gluttons for punishment. Former *Good Morning America* anchor, Joan Lunden, is a perfect example. Although the 52-year-old celebrity already has three daughters from a previous marriage (ages 22, 20, and 15), she developed a burning desire to have a child with her current husband, Jeff Konigsberg. Because there was absolutely no way Mother Nature was going to participate in this venture, Joan and her husband worked out an arrangement with a surrogate mother. Joan wrote a big check, a team of doctors worked their magic, and nine months later the surrogate gave birth to twins, Kate and Max. I just have one thing to say about all of this. Joan, HAVE YOU LOST YOUR EVER-LOVIN' MIND? Ms. Lunden will be 70 years old when the new bundles of joy graduate from high school. Seventy! Then poor Joan will be forced to deal with two college freshmen when she should be focusing her attention on getting enough fiber in her diet. Suddenly, I don't feel so bad about my situation.

A couple of days ago, I was in the Sears store at Fair Oaks Mall, shopping for an air filter for my lawn mower (I lead such a glamorous life). I noticed a man standing next to the riding mowers, holding a little girl who appeared to be about two years old. The man was looking at me as if he knew me. As I walked in his direction, I realized he was an old friend, Brody Ellsworth, from my home town. We had a few classes together in high school, and I always considered him to be a good friend. After we graduated, I went to Virginia Tech and he went to James Madison University. Unfortunately, we lost touch and hadn't seen each other in 24 years. I asked Brody, "What's your daughter's name?"

"This beautiful little girl is Kayla, but she's not my daughter; she's my granddaughter. I married Jennifer Russell when I was 19. Nine months later, we had our first daughter, Kira. She got married when she was 18 and had Kayla a couple of years later."

"Brody, you're a grandfather? Wow!"

"Yeah, it's great. She's my pride and joy. I love being a grandpa." Grandpa? Can a guy my age be considered a grandpa? I thought that name was reserved for

80-year-old men who smell like Old Spice, hoard Werther's Original Candy, and give you silver dollars on your birthday.

Brody had to go meet his wife for lunch, so he said goodbye and walked away with little Kayla toddling by his side. I watched them pass through the door into the mall, and I felt glad Brody was so happy to be a grandfather. I felt even better about the fact that I am not a grandpa yet. I'm still a vibrant young man, on a journey to find action and excitement. I celebrated my youth by dancing through the power tool department singing, "One Bad Apple."

Myths, Old Wives' Tales, and the Truth

As you travel through the confusing maze of parenthood, you hear all kinds of goofy myths that get mixed in with useful facts. How do you tell the difference between an old wives' tale and a useful piece of substantiated information? No, you don't need to rummage through thousands of Google search results to find the truth. I have combed the Internet for you and assembled a compilation of data that dispels common myths and old wives' tales with genuine, indisputable truths that I just made up. Here we go.

Myth: All women look beautiful when they're pregnant.

The Truth: Contrary to popular belief, spider veins, acne, ankles the size of watermelons, dramatic mood swings, and 40 extra pounds do not make a woman beautiful. I know, some pregnant women seem to "glow," but don't kid yourself. That's just sweat from walking up a flight of stairs to go to the bathroom for the 38th time in three hours. Let's conduct a little comparison: a woman who is eight months pregnant vs. the stunning Halle Berry. Which one is more beautiful? You be the judge and be honest. The truth is, no woman on Earth can really look gorgeous when she is "with child," except for my lovely wife, Starla. Yes, I am sucking up. I want a big screen TV for Christmas, and I need all the brownie points I can get.

Myth: Women's feet grow a full size during pregnancy.

The Truth: Our experience has shown that this statement is entirely true. When she was pregnant with Chase, Starla totaled her favorite pair of Reeboks. The shoes were declared to be in a "state of emergency" by the governor of Virginia. Unfortunately, the sneakers did not survive the painful ordeal and were cremated. After a lovely parting ceremony, we spread their ashes over the floor of the aerobics room of our gym. The manager got mad and made us sweep them up. That man has no compassion.

Myth: A cat can suck the breath out of babies while they are asleep.

The Truth: This is just a silly old wives' tale. I assure you, cats do not have the ability to suck the life out of young children. If you hear unusual noises coming from your child's bedroom, it is not the sound of a cat trying to steal your kid's life force. It is a little known fact that cats like to gather together late at night, put on elaborate costumes, and perform classic Broadway musicals. Their favorites are *Annie Get Your Gun, Hello Dolly, South Pacific,* and *Oklahoma.* Just in case you are wondering, no, they do not put on productions of Andrew Lloyd Webber's popular musical *Cats* because that would be too cliché.

Myth: A magic stone protects Saddam Hussein from harm.

The Truth: *The Christian Science Monitor* reports that many people in Iraq believe Saddam Hussein has shrouded himself with dark powers. In an interview with a reporter, an Iraqi car dealer describes a "magic stone" that some are convinced renders the dictator-in-hiding indestructible. "First of all, he put the stone on a chicken and tried to shoot it. Then he put it on a cow, and the bullets went around it," the car dealer said. Children around the world will discover the real truth behind this urban legend when they read J. K. Rowling's next book, which is titled *Harry Potter and the Whackjob Dictator's Magic Stone.*

Myth: If you cross your eyes, they'll stick that way.

The Truth: This is absolutely true. Stop it. Right now. I mean it.

Myth: Breaking a mirror brings seven years of bad luck.

The Truth: Nope. Not true. Breaking a mirror has no connection to bad luck; however, if you break your wife's beloved antique mirror with a football, she will remind you of your ghastly offense every day for the rest of your miserable life. Seven years of bad luck doesn't sound so bad now, does it?

Myth: Santa Claus employs more than 4,000 elves who work in a huge toy factory.

The Truth: For many decades, Santa owned and operated an enormous toy factory at the North Pole Toy Company. Labor costs increased exponentially in the '80s and managing 4,000 rowdy elves became a real headache. In the early '90s, Santa decided to outsource his toy manufacturing processes to Mattel, Hasbro, Lego, and Sony. This idea proved to be so successful that he outsourced all of his call center operations to Accenture, and his information technology department is now run by IBM. A few of the elves transitioned their employment from the North Pole Toy Company to Mattel and Sony. The rest of the elves cashed in their stock options and retired to a lovely planned community in Boca Raton, Florida.

Myth: Sitting too close to the TV will damage your eyes.

The Truth: The American Academy of Ophthalmology says children have the ability to focus at close distances without eyestrain; consequently, they often develop the habit of sitting directly in front of the television. Parents, there's no need to worry if your kids like to sit very close to the TV. But if your children like to watch *The Osbournes,* you should worry.

Myth: You should not go swimming for an hour after you eat.

The Truth: In the August 1992 issue of the *Berkeley Wellness Letter,* Dr. Ernest Maglischo, the swimming coach at California State University at Bakersfield, claims marathon swimmers often eat high carbohydrate meals before swimming. Don't sweat the eating and swimming situation. This problem is not the biggest one you'll have to deal with at the pool. After you spend three hours getting your kids ready to go swimming, you'll lug more than 900 pounds of sunscreen, toys, water shoes, floaties, life vests, and snacks to a broken lounge chair at the side of the pool. Approximately 24 seconds after your three-year-old jumps into the water, he will look at you in alarm and scream, "I HAVE TO POOOOOOOOOP." You will rush him into the locker room where the air conditioning unit will be set on "Arctic." The frigid air will magically make the poop disappear. So you traipse back to the pool with your three-year-old in tow. Four minutes later, the poop returns, bigger and badder than ever. You race your kid back to the locker room, but now the poop has developed a mind of its own. Your son lets out a piercing yell as the insurgent poop escapes from its biological penitentiary. For the next 35 minutes, you'll clean up your kid, the locker room floor, and a shower stall. As your three-year-old emerges from the locker room wearing a new pair of swim trunks, he'll turn to you and say, "Can we go home now?" You'll just shake your head, pack up your load of swimming paraphernalia, and head to your car. Another fun-filled day at the pool has come to an end.

Myth: Raising children will make your hair turn gray.

The Truth: Hair turns gray because pigment cells in the hair base at the roots of the hair stop producing melanin. Fair-haired and dark-haired people have equal chances of getting gray hair. The graying of hair is thought to be genetically determined; however, telling your kids to pick up their socks 11 gazillion times seems to accelerate the graying process.

I hope this information is useful to you. Call me if you have any questions. Oh, my gosh, it's getting late. I have to go. Our neighborhood cat troupe is putting on a rousing production of *My Fair Lady,* and the show is about to start. Talk to you later.

A Letter to My Sons

As fathers, we are compelled to work our butts off to provide our children with food, clothing, and shelter. We expend a great deal of time and an enormous amount of effort to give our children the things we never had when we were kids. Many dads show love for their children by giving them the coolest toys on the market, sending them to exclusive schools, or living in the biggest house they can afford.

Unfortunately, our pursuit of money severely hinders our ability to build close relationships with our kids. We work 16-hour days so we can make more money. On weekends and holidays, we trudge to our offices so we can impress our bosses and earn promotions. Even when we are supposed to be on family vacations, we join marathon conference calls so we can close big deals and land big bonus checks. In my long and not-so-illustrious professional career, I have done all of these things, but I'm not going to do them anymore.

I know men are defined by their careers, and I understand how important it is to be successful in your chosen field of work, but have you ever thought about the fact that a massive majority of the work you produce on a daily basis is disposable? Think about the projects you slaved over a year ago. How many of those projects are now completely irrelevant? What about the work that consumed almost every waking hour of your life five years ago? Ten years ago? How much of that work is still applicable today? I'm guessing your answer is—very little. It kills me to think that I squandered so much precious time working on immaterial projects when I should have spent that time with my family.

After seven years of fatherhood, I've come to the following conclusion: the most significant gift you can give your child is your time. Your kid doesn't care about money, he or she cares about you. Although a kid may nag incessantly for a new bike or the latest PlayStation game, in reality, your child actually craves your time. It doesn't matter if it's a day at the beach or a simple game of checkers, your child just wants to be with you.

Most important, take time to tell your children how you feel about them. I'm well aware of the fact that men find it difficult to express their feelings, but you have to let your children know how much you care about them. They need to hear it, and you need to say it. If you have difficulty articulating your thoughts verbally, write a letter to your child. Below you will see a letter I wrote to my sons, Chase and Logan. This was my way of telling my boys that they mean the world to me and I'm proud to be their dad.

Dear Chase and Logan,

My dad passed away long before you were born. Twenty years ago, he developed prostate cancer and died before his time. Dad would have gotten a real kick out of you guys. He was very funny. I got his sense of humor. So did you.

Dad took pride in being a simple man. He had to drop out of school after the eighth grade to help support his family during the Depression. Growing up in the Blue Ridge Mountains of Virginia was difficult in the '20s and '30s, but he never complained about being a dirt-poor kid. After he fought in World War II, he became a carpenter and settled down to become a traditional family man. He never wanted to be a high-powered business executive. Dad had his own measure of success. He aspired to work hard Monday through Friday, watch baseball games on Saturday afternoon, and go to church every Sunday morning with his family. That was enough for him.

We argued constantly. I don't know why. We disagreed about everything from music to religion to Reggie Jackson's batting stance. Maybe both of us were incredibly hardheaded, or maybe we were from vastly different generations. The reason doesn't matter. I know he loved me and I loved him, but we just couldn't find a way to live with each other peacefully. The biggest regret of my life is that our continuous bickering severely damaged our relationship, and I will never have an opportunity to fix it. All I can do now is make sure I don't make the same mistake with you.

Before you were born, I stumbled through my adult life without a clear direction. I lived from year to year, pretending to build a professional career that was ordinary at its highest point. Thankfully, you guys came along to help me find my way out of a murky existence. At some point in his life, a man has to decide what is most important to him. For me, it's my family—everything else is insignificant. I don't care if I never become the chief marketing officer of a huge multinational conglomerate or a fabulously rich entrepreneur with a home in the Hamptons. I want to watch you turn a double play in a little league baseball game and see your face light up as you dive into an ice cream sundae on a hot summer afternoon. That's enough for me.

I'm sure you've noticed that I'm not a perfect man. I have more faults than I care to mention. Although I know I'll make thousands of mistakes over the years, I promise I'll work as hard as I possibly can to take care of you, spend time with you, listen to your opinions, and help you grow up to be strong, honorable men. I'll treasure every moment I spend with you.

As long as you live, I want you to remember two things about me: I'm proud of you, and I will always love you.

Dad

P.S. Pick up your socks.

About the Author

Dale Alderman lives in Chantilly, Virginia with his wife, Starla, and two sons, Chase and Logan. He barely graduated from Virginia Tech in 1984 and somehow convinced Marymount University to give him a master's degree in 1995. For 19 years, he worked as a sales and marketing executive for large global corporations, and then he decided to get a real life and spend time with his family. In his spare time, he avoids going to the gym, feeds his addiction to chocolate, and watches movies with his kids.

0-595-29617-3

CPSIA information can be obtained at www.ICGtesting.com
Printed in the USA
LVOW07s2010111114

413137LV00001B/265/P